# The History o

# Echoes of the Outback

Copyright © 2023 by Charlotte Chambers-Brown and Einar Felix Hansen.

All rights reserved. No part of this publication may be reproduced, stored in a retrieval system, or transmitted, in any form or by any means, electronic, mechanical, photocopying, recording, or otherwise, without the prior written permission of the copyright holder. This book was created with the help of Artificial Intelligence technology.

The contents of this book are intended for entertainment purposes only. While every effort has been made to ensure the accuracy and reliability of the information presented, the author and publisher make no warranties or representations as to the accuracy, completeness, or suitability of the information contained herein. The information presented in this book is not intended as a substitute for professional advice, and readers should consult with qualified professionals in the relevant fields for specific advice.

The Ancient Land Down Under: Origins and Indigenous Cultures 7

Dreamtime and Aboriginal Australia: Myth, Legend, and Belief Systems 10

The First Settlers: European Exploration and Early Contact 13

Terra Australis Incognita: The Quest for the Great Southern Land 16

Captain James Cook and the Discovery of the East Coast 19

The First Fleet: Convicts and Colonization 22

Early Struggles: Life in the Penal Colony 25

The Gold Rush Era: Boom and Bust 28

Bushrangers and Outlaws: Tales of Crime and Infamy 31

Federation and the Birth of Modern Australia 34

World War I: Australia's Sacrifice and Nationhood 37

The Roaring Twenties: Social Change and Economic Growth 40

The Great Depression: Hardship and Resilience 43

World War II: Australia on the Frontline 46

Post-War Reconstruction: A Nation Rebuilds 49

The Snowy Mountains Scheme: Engineering Marvel of the South 53

The Stolen Generations: Dark Chapter in Australia's History 56

Indigenous Rights and Reconciliation: The Road to Healing 59

From White Australia to Multiculturalism: Immigration and Identity 63

Mateship and the Anzac Spirit: Australia's Military Legacy 66

Women's Suffrage and the Fight for Equality 69

Indigenous Land Rights: Struggles and Achievements 72

The Whitlam Years: Progressive Politics and Social Reform 76

Bicentenary Celebrations: Reflecting on Two Hundred Years 79

Sydney Opera House: Icon of Modern Australia 82

The Great Barrier Reef: Underwater Wonderland 85

Kangaroos, Koalas, and Wombats: Australia's Unique Wildlife 88

Aboriginal Art and Culture: Ancient Traditions, Modern Expressions 91

Ayers Rock (Uluru): Sacred Heart of Australia 94

**The Outback: Vast Deserts and Remote Landscapes 97**

**The Sydney Harbour Bridge: An Engineering Triumph 100**

**Melbourne: From Gold Rush Town to Cultural Capital 103**

**The Great Ocean Road: Scenic Beauty on Australia's Coastline 106**

**The Blue Mountains: Majestic Wilderness Near Sydney 109**

**The Whitsunday Islands: Paradise in the Coral Sea 112**

**Tasmania: Untamed Wilderness and Historic Heritage 115**

**Australia Today: Challenges, Achievements, and the Road Ahead 119**

**Conclusion 122**

# The Ancient Land Down Under: Origins and Indigenous Cultures

Australia, known as the "Land Down Under," is a vast continent with a rich and ancient history. The origins of human habitation in Australia can be traced back tens of thousands of years, making it one of the oldest continuously inhabited regions on Earth. The continent's indigenous cultures have flourished for countless generations, adapting to diverse environments and leaving a lasting impact on the land and its people.

The history of Australia's indigenous cultures begins with the Aboriginal peoples, who are believed to have migrated to the continent from Southeast Asia over 65,000 years ago. These diverse groups of hunter-gatherers developed unique cultures and deep connections with the land, evolving intricate knowledge and spiritual beliefs closely intertwined with their environment.

The Aboriginal people developed a profound understanding of the Australian landscape, harnessing its resources for sustenance and survival. They developed sophisticated methods of hunting, fishing, and gathering, adapting their practices to the diverse ecosystems they encountered across the continent. The knowledge of the land and its resources was passed down through generations, forming the basis of their rich cultural heritage.

Australia's indigenous cultures are incredibly diverse, with hundreds of distinct language groups and cultural traditions. Each group had its own unique customs, rituals, and artistic expressions, reflecting the richness and diversity of their ancestral connections to the land. Art played a significant role in indigenous cultures, with rock paintings, engravings, and ceremonial objects showcasing intricate designs and profound spiritual meanings.

Spirituality and the Dreamtime are fundamental aspects of Aboriginal belief systems. The Dreamtime refers to the creation period when ancestral beings shaped the landscape and laid the foundations of cultural practices. Aboriginal people believe that the land, waterways, and celestial bodies are imbued with the spirit of these ancestral beings, forming a spiritual connection that shapes their identity and worldview.

Throughout history, Aboriginal societies were organized into complex kinship systems, with social structures and responsibilities governed by intricate relationships between family groups. These systems facilitated cooperation, trade, and the exchange of knowledge between different communities.

The arrival of Europeans in the late 18th century marked a significant turning point in the history of Australia's indigenous cultures. The impact of colonization was profound, leading to devastating consequences for Aboriginal communities. The dispossession of land, the introduction of new diseases, and violent conflicts disrupted and displaced indigenous populations, causing significant social and cultural upheaval.

Despite the immense challenges faced by indigenous communities, their resilience and cultural strength have endured. Efforts towards reconciliation and recognition of indigenous rights have gained momentum in recent decades, with steps taken to address past injustices and promote cultural preservation and empowerment.

Today, Australia's indigenous cultures continue to thrive, with vibrant artistic traditions, ongoing connections to the land, and a growing appreciation for the importance of indigenous knowledge systems. Efforts to promote cultural diversity and foster a deeper understanding of indigenous histories and contributions are integral to Australia's national identity and the ongoing process of reconciliation.

The ancient origins and enduring presence of Australia's indigenous cultures serve as a testament to the depth of human history on this vast continent. Understanding and valuing the unique perspectives and contributions of indigenous Australians is crucial for appreciating the complete narrative of Australia's history and embracing a more inclusive and equitable future.

# Dreamtime and Aboriginal Australia: Myth, Legend, and Belief Systems

Within the rich tapestry of Aboriginal Australia, the Dreamtime holds a profound significance. It represents a complex and spiritual realm where mythology, creation stories, and ancestral beings intertwine to form the foundation of Aboriginal belief systems. The Dreamtime is not merely a concept; it is a living, ever-present force that shapes the cultural and spiritual identity of Aboriginal peoples.

At the core of Aboriginal belief systems is the understanding that the Dreamtime is not a distant past but a continuous reality that exists alongside the present. It is a timeless dimension where ancestral beings shaped the land, the animals, and the laws that govern human behavior. The Dreamtime is inseparable from the physical world and provides a framework through which Aboriginal peoples understand and interact with their environment.

In Aboriginal mythology, ancestral beings, often referred to as "Dreamtime beings" or "totemic ancestors," emerged from the land, the sea, and the sky. These powerful beings took various forms, ranging from animals and plants to celestial bodies and natural elements. Each ancestral being played a specific role in shaping the landscape and establishing cultural practices.

Creation stories within the Dreamtime describe how these ancestral beings traveled across the land, leaving their mark through song, dance, and other artistic expressions. These stories serve as both a historical record and a moral guide, teaching important lessons about human behavior, relationships, and the consequences of actions.

Aboriginal mythology is as diverse as the landscape itself, with different regions and language groups having their unique stories and interpretations of the Dreamtime. The stories often explain natural phenomena, the origins of specific landmarks, and the creation of different animal species. They offer insights into the interconnectedness of all aspects of existence and emphasize the importance of living in harmony with the land and its inhabitants.

Art plays a crucial role in expressing and preserving the Dreamtime narratives. Rock art, cave paintings, and ceremonial objects are adorned with symbols and motifs representing ancestral beings and their journeys. These artistic expressions are not mere decorations but visual representations of profound spiritual beliefs and cultural practices.

Ceremonies and rituals form an integral part of Aboriginal cultural life, providing a means to connect with the Dreamtime and reinforce ancestral connections. Song, dance, storytelling, and body painting are essential components of these ceremonies, enabling participants to engage with the Dreamtime and seek guidance from the ancestral beings.

It is important to note that Aboriginal belief systems and the Dreamtime are not homogenous across all communities. While there are overarching themes and shared elements, there is considerable diversity in the stories, rituals, and interpretations of the Dreamtime. Different language groups and regions have their unique cosmologies and traditions, reflecting the diversity and complexity of Aboriginal cultures.

The Dreamtime continues to shape the lives of Aboriginal peoples today. It informs their relationships with the land, their spiritual practices, and their sense of identity. The preservation and promotion of the Dreamtime narratives and cultural practices are essential for the well-being and cultural resilience of Aboriginal communities.

Understanding and appreciating the Dreamtime is an invitation to explore the depth and richness of Aboriginal Australia's cultural heritage. It allows us to engage with a worldview that values the interconnectedness of all life, the power of storytelling, and the enduring legacy of ancestral beings. By embracing the myths, legends, and belief systems of Aboriginal Australia, we gain a deeper appreciation for the spiritual and cultural tapestry that has shaped this ancient land for millennia.

# The First Settlers: European Exploration and Early Contact

The history of European exploration and early contact with Australia is a fascinating chapter in the story of this vast continent. It was during the 17th and 18th centuries that European nations embarked on voyages of discovery, driven by curiosity, the quest for wealth, and the desire to expand their empires. The encounters between European explorers and the indigenous peoples of Australia marked the beginning of a new era for the continent.

One of the first recorded European explorations of Australia was undertaken by Dutch navigator Willem Janszoon in 1606. Sailing aboard the Duyfken, Janszoon landed on the western coast of Cape York Peninsula in what is now Queensland. This marked the first known European contact with the Australian continent, although the Dutch did not establish any permanent settlements at the time.

Over a century later, the renowned British explorer, Captain James Cook, arrived on the eastern coast of Australia in 1770. His expedition aboard the HM Bark Endeavour was commissioned by the Royal Society to observe the transit of Venus and explore the lands of the Southern Hemisphere. Cook's landing at Botany Bay (now part of Sydney) opened the way for future British colonization.

In 1778, the British government sent the First Fleet, led by Captain Arthur Phillip, to establish a penal colony in Australia. The fleet consisted of 11 ships carrying around

1,400 people, including convicts, marines, and officers. On January 26, 1788, the First Fleet arrived at Port Jackson (now Sydney Harbour) and established the settlement of New South Wales. This date is commemorated as Australia Day, a national holiday.

The early years of the colony were challenging, as the settlers faced numerous hardships, including unfamiliar environments, limited resources, and conflicts with the indigenous peoples. The convicts, many of whom were sent to Australia for relatively minor offenses, were tasked with building infrastructure and cultivating the land under the watchful eye of the military forces.

As European settlement expanded, interactions between the newcomers and the indigenous peoples varied. In some instances, there were clashes and misunderstandings, leading to violence and displacement. The dispossession of indigenous lands and the introduction of diseases had a devastating impact on Aboriginal communities.

European exploration and settlement also brought significant changes to the natural environment. The introduction of new plant and animal species, such as livestock and European crops, had both positive and negative effects on the Australian ecosystem. The arrival of European diseases, like smallpox, had a devastating impact on the indigenous population, who had no immunity to these illnesses.

As more British colonies were established in different parts of Australia, including Tasmania, South Australia, Western Australia, and Victoria, the continent became further integrated into the expanding British Empire. The discovery of gold in the mid-19th century sparked significant population growth and economic development, attracting immigrants from around the world and transforming the colonies into thriving communities.

The early contacts between European explorers and the indigenous peoples of Australia had profound and enduring consequences. The impact of colonization on Aboriginal cultures, languages, and land rights cannot be overlooked. Understanding and acknowledging this complex history are vital steps toward reconciliation and promoting a more inclusive and equitable society.

The exploration and settlement of Australia by Europeans laid the foundations for the modern nation. It is a history marked by both achievements and challenges, shaping the diverse and multicultural society that Australia is today. Exploring this chapter of Australian history offers valuable insights into the complexities of human interactions, the impacts of colonization, and the ongoing efforts to recognize and reconcile the past.

# Terra Australis Incognita: The Quest for the Great Southern Land

The quest for the Great Southern Land, also known as Terra Australis Incognita, captivated the minds and ambitions of European explorers during the Age of Discovery. Inspired by ancient theories and fueled by a desire for riches, knowledge, and territorial expansion, numerous expeditions were launched in search of this elusive southern continent.

The concept of Terra Australis can be traced back to ancient Greek and Roman geographers who hypothesized the existence of a vast southern landmass to balance the northern hemisphere. This theoretical land was believed to be rich in resources and knowledge, thus attracting the attention of explorers in subsequent centuries.

One of the earliest European attempts to find Terra Australis was made by Portuguese navigators in the 16th century. Explorers such as Cristóvão de Mendonça and Pedro Fernandes de Queirós embarked on expeditions across the Pacific Ocean, hoping to discover the fabled southern continent. While these voyages did not lead to the discovery of Terra Australis, they contributed to a growing body of knowledge about the Pacific and its islands.

Dutch explorers played a significant role in the quest for the Great Southern Land. In 1606, Willem Janszoon became the first recorded European to set foot on Australian soil during his expedition along the west coast of Cape York Peninsula. Subsequent Dutch explorers, including Dirk Hartog, Abel Tasman, and William

Dampier, charted parts of the Australian coastline and made important contributions to early European understanding of the continent.

The British also became engaged in the search for Terra Australis. Captain James Cook's voyage aboard the HMS Endeavour in 1768 was primarily focused on observing the transit of Venus and exploring the Pacific, but it also carried a secret mission to search for the southern land. Cook's exploration of the eastern coastline of Australia in 1770 revealed the continent's vastness and potential for colonization.

The quest for Terra Australis was not solely driven by dreams of wealth and expansion. European explorers also sought scientific knowledge and advancements in cartography, astronomy, and natural history. The observations and discoveries made during these voyages greatly contributed to the understanding of navigation, geography, and the natural sciences.

It is important to note that the search for Terra Australis was not a unified endeavor, but rather a collective effort involving multiple nations and explorers. While the idea of a southern continent persisted, the actual landmass that was discovered and explored gradually deviated from the original concept of Terra Australis. The term "Australia" was eventually used to refer to the continent, which was officially named New South Wales by Captain Cook.

The quest for the Great Southern Land represents a remarkable chapter in the history of exploration and discovery. The expeditions undertaken by European navigators shaped the world's understanding of geography, expanded the known boundaries of the planet, and laid the groundwork for future colonization and interaction between Europe and Australia.

Although Terra Australis as envisioned by ancient geographers was not found, the exploration of Australia opened up new horizons and opportunities for scientific, economic, and cultural exchange. The encounters between European explorers and the indigenous peoples of Australia, though marked by tensions and conflict, became an integral part of the continent's complex history.

The quest for Terra Australis Incognita is a testament to the human spirit of curiosity, adventure, and the pursuit of knowledge. It serves as a reminder of the transformative power of exploration and its lasting impact on the course of history. The journeys of these intrepid explorers laid the foundations for the future development and settlement of the vast and diverse continent of Australia.

# Captain James Cook and the Discovery of the East Coast

Captain James Cook's voyage to the East Coast of Australia in 1770 is a pivotal moment in the history of exploration and the European discovery of the continent. Commissioned by the Royal Society and the British Admiralty, Cook's expedition aboard the HMS Endeavour sought to accomplish scientific, navigational, and geographic objectives while unraveling the mysteries of the vast Pacific Ocean.

Setting sail from Plymouth, England, on August 26, 1768, Cook's journey had several important objectives. One of the primary goals was to observe the transit of Venus, a rare celestial event that could provide valuable data for astronomers and help refine calculations of the Earth's distance from the Sun. Another objective was to explore the Pacific region and potentially find the elusive southern continent, known as Terra Australis.

After making stops in Brazil, Tahiti, and New Zealand, Cook's ship, the HMS Endeavour, reached the eastern coast of Australia in April 1770. The crew encountered unfamiliar shores and encountered the indigenous people who inhabited the land. Cook named the area "New South Wales" in honor of the region's resemblance to the Welsh landscape.

Cook's meticulous charting of the coastline, along with detailed observations and recordings, significantly contributed to the understanding of Australia's geography and natural features. He meticulously recorded his findings, including the intricate details of the coastline, the flora and fauna, and the interactions with the Aboriginal peoples he encountered along the way.

During his exploration of the eastern coast, Cook and his crew made significant landings at sites such as Botany Bay, where they encountered a diverse range of plant species that fascinated the botanists aboard the ship. The expedition continued northward, with Cook charting and naming landmarks, including Cape Tribulation, the Great Barrier Reef, and the Endeavour River, where the ship underwent repairs.

Throughout the journey, Cook and his crew had numerous interactions with the Aboriginal peoples they encountered. These encounters varied from friendly exchanges to tense conflicts, highlighting the challenges of cross-cultural communication and the complexities of cultural differences. Cook's approach towards indigenous peoples, although influenced by the prevailing attitudes of the time, was generally characterized by a mixture of curiosity, respect, and a desire to establish peaceful relations.

Cook's voyage on the Endeavour ultimately circumnavigated the globe, returning to England in July 1771. The wealth of scientific data, including the detailed charts and observations made during the exploration of the eastern coast of Australia, greatly contributed to the knowledge and understanding of the Pacific region. Cook's accurate mapping of the coastline laid the groundwork for future explorations, colonization, and the establishment of British settlements on the eastern seaboard.

The significance of Cook's exploration cannot be overstated. His voyages opened up new possibilities for trade, colonization, and scientific inquiry. The observations and charts produced during the expedition provided a foundation for subsequent voyages and played a crucial role in the eventual British colonization of Australia.

It is important to acknowledge that Cook's expeditions, like those of other European explorers of the time, had lasting impacts on the indigenous peoples of Australia. The encounters with Cook and his crew brought significant changes to the lives of Aboriginal communities, including the introduction of new diseases, displacement from traditional lands, and the disruption of cultural practices.

Captain James Cook's exploration of the East Coast of Australia stands as a testament to human curiosity, scientific inquiry, and the drive to expand geographical knowledge. His meticulous observations, accurate charts, and encounters with the indigenous peoples of Australia continue to shape our understanding of the continent's history and cultural heritage. Cook's legacy, while complex and multifaceted, forms an integral part of Australia's national narrative and the ongoing process of reconciliation between indigenous and non-indigenous Australians.

# The First Fleet: Convicts and Colonization

The arrival of the First Fleet in Australia in 1788 marked a significant turning point in the history of the continent. The fleet, consisting of 11 ships, was dispatched by the British government with the primary purpose of establishing a penal colony in New South Wales.

The decision to establish a convict settlement in Australia was influenced by several factors. Britain, facing overcrowded prisons and a growing population of convicts, sought an alternative solution to alleviate the strain on its penal system. The idea of sending convicts to a distant land provided an opportunity for both punishment and potential colonization.

On May 13, 1787, the First Fleet departed from Portsmouth, England, under the command of Captain Arthur Phillip. On board were approximately 1,400 people, including convicts, marines, officers, and their families. The convicts, numbering around 700 men and 200 women, were primarily sent for offenses considered serious by the standards of the time, ranging from theft to more severe crimes.

After a grueling voyage lasting over eight months, the First Fleet arrived at Botany Bay on January 18, 1788. However, the area was deemed unsuitable for settlement due to poor soil and a lack of fresh water. Captain Phillip, accompanied by a small group, explored further north and discovered Port Jackson, an area that offered better natural resources and the potential for a secure harbor. On January 26, 1788, the British raised the Union Jack and established the settlement of Sydney Cove, which later became Sydney, the capital of New South Wales.

The early years of the colony were marked by numerous challenges. The convicts and the free settlers faced difficulties in adapting to the unfamiliar environment. The harsh climate, limited resources, and the need to establish infrastructure from scratch presented significant obstacles. Food shortages, disease, and conflicts with the indigenous peoples further added to the hardships faced by the settlers.

The colony was primarily intended as a place of punishment and reformation for the convicts. They were put to work building the necessary infrastructure, clearing land for agriculture, and constructing the first buildings of the settlement. Punishments, including floggings and time in chains, were employed as means of discipline.

As the colony grew, efforts were made to establish a more structured society. Free settlers arrived, and land grants were given to encourage agriculture and economic development. The establishment of a legal system, schools, and churches further contributed to the growing sense of community and stability.

The impact of colonization on the indigenous peoples of Australia cannot be ignored. As British settlement expanded, conflicts arose between the colonists and the Aboriginal communities, leading to violence and the displacement of indigenous populations from their traditional lands. The introduction of new diseases further devastated Aboriginal communities, who had little immunity to these illnesses.

Over time, the penal colony began to transform into a more diverse society as both convicts and free settlers were granted conditional pardons or served their sentences. The economy developed through agriculture, with crops such as wheat, barley, and vegetables being cultivated, and sheep and cattle farming being established.

The establishment of the penal colony in Australia was not without controversy. The impact on the indigenous peoples, the use of convict labor, and the social inequalities that developed within the colony were subjects of debate and criticism. However, it is important to understand the events of the time within the context of the prevailing attitudes and practices of the 18th century.

The arrival of the First Fleet marked the beginning of a new chapter in Australia's history, as European colonization took root on the continent. The establishment of Sydney as a settlement laid the foundations for future British colonies and the eventual formation of the nation of Australia.

The legacy of the First Fleet and the convict era continues to shape Australia's national identity and cultural heritage. The stories of resilience, survival, and adaptation of the early settlers, both convict and free, contribute to the collective narrative of a nation built on diversity and determination.

# Early Struggles: Life in the Penal Colony

The early years of the penal colony in Australia were marked by numerous challenges, hardships, and struggles. Life in the colony was characterized by a unique blend of punishment, adaptation, and the efforts of both convicts and free settlers to establish a functioning society in an unfamiliar and often hostile environment.

Upon arrival in the colony, convicts faced a stark and unforgiving reality. The harsh climate, unfamiliar landscapes, and limited resources posed significant challenges to survival. The early settlements, including Sydney Cove, were primitive and lacked the necessary infrastructure and amenities for comfortable living.

Food shortages were a recurring issue in the early years of the colony. The unfamiliar soil and climate made agriculture difficult, and initial attempts at farming were met with limited success. The scarcity of fresh water and the absence of reliable food sources led to periods of hunger and malnutrition among the settlers.

The convicts, comprising the majority of the population in the early years, were subjected to strict discipline and punishment. The penal system aimed to reform and deter through harsh measures. Floggings, solitary confinement, and hard labor were common forms of punishment for both minor infractions and more serious offenses.

The convict labor force played a vital role in building the infrastructure of the colony. Under the supervision of military and civilian authorities, convicts were assigned tasks such as constructing buildings, clearing land, and working on public works projects. Their labor was instrumental in shaping the physical landscape of the colony and establishing the foundations for future development.

Social dynamics within the colony were complex. The hierarchical structure, with military and administrative officials at the top, created divisions between convicts, free settlers, and the ruling class. Social mobility was limited, and the stigma associated with convict status often endured even after serving a sentence or receiving a pardon.

The interactions between the colonists and the indigenous peoples varied. Initial encounters were often marked by curiosity and exchanges of goods, but as the colony expanded, conflicts arose over land, resources, and cultural misunderstandings. These conflicts resulted in violence and strained relationships between the two groups.

The early years of the penal colony were plagued by disease and health challenges. Poor sanitation, crowded living conditions, and the introduction of new diseases had a devastating impact on the settlers and the indigenous populations. Outbreaks of smallpox and other illnesses further disrupted daily life and had severe consequences for the affected communities.

Despite these challenges, efforts were made to establish a functioning society. The legal system was gradually implemented, providing a framework for justice and governance. Schools and churches were established, contributing to the development of social and cultural institutions within the colony.

As time passed, the colony began to evolve and adapt. Agriculture improved, with new farming techniques and crops leading to increased food production. Trade with other British colonies and interactions with visiting ships brought new supplies and opportunities for commerce.

The struggles and hardships faced by the early settlers, both convicts and free settlers, played a significant role in shaping the character and resilience of the emerging Australian society. The experiences of survival, adaptation, and perseverance laid the foundations for the diverse and multicultural nation that Australia is today.

It is essential to approach the early struggles of the penal colony with an understanding of the context and prevailing attitudes of the time. The penal system and the challenges faced by the settlers should be viewed within the broader historical framework, acknowledging the complexities and contradictions inherent in the establishment of a convict colony.

The legacy of the early struggles in the penal colony continues to resonate in Australian society. It serves as a reminder of the resilience, resourcefulness, and determination of the early settlers. Examining this chapter of history provides insights into the complexities of human experience, the impact of colonization, and the ongoing journey toward reconciliation and understanding.

# The Gold Rush Era: Boom and Bust

The Gold Rush era in Australia, which began in the mid-19th century, was a transformative period in the nation's history. It brought an influx of fortune-seekers from around the world, generated economic growth, and contributed to the development of towns and infrastructure. However, it also had its share of challenges and societal impacts.

The discovery of gold in Australia sparked a frenzy that attracted thousands of prospectors hoping to strike it rich. The first significant gold find occurred in New South Wales in 1851, followed by discoveries in Victoria, Queensland, Western Australia, and other regions. News of the gold rushes spread rapidly, leading to a surge in population and the rapid growth of mining settlements.

The lure of gold brought people from diverse backgrounds to the Australian colonies. Immigrants arrived from countries such as China, Ireland, England, Germany, and America, seeking their fortune in the goldfields. This influx of people created a melting pot of cultures, languages, and customs, contributing to the multicultural fabric of Australian society.

The gold rushes had a profound impact on the economy of Australia. Mining became a major industry, driving economic growth and providing employment opportunities. The influx of wealth from gold exports helped to stimulate the local economies and fund infrastructure projects, including the construction of roads, railways, and public buildings.

Mining techniques and technologies rapidly evolved during the gold rush era. Initially, shallow alluvial mining was the dominant method, with miners panning for gold in rivers and streams. As the easily accessible gold deposits were depleted, more complex and industrialized methods, such as deep shaft mining and hydraulic sluicing, were employed.

The goldfields became bustling communities with their own social structures and institutions. Camps and townships sprang up, catering to the needs of the miners and their families. General stores, hotels, banks, and entertainment venues emerged, providing essential services and creating opportunities for entrepreneurs and businesses.

The gold rush era was not without its challenges. Living and working conditions on the goldfields were often harsh and demanding. Miners faced long hours, physical labor, and exposure to the elements. Law and order were sometimes difficult to maintain, leading to instances of crime and disputes over mining claims.

The societal impacts of the gold rush era were far-reaching. The population boom led to increased demand for housing, food, and basic necessities. The influx of immigrants, particularly the large numbers of Chinese miners, created tensions and cultural clashes within the communities. Discrimination and racism were prevalent, reflecting the attitudes and prejudices of the time.

The gold rush era was characterized by periods of boom and bust. Initially, the discovery of gold brought great excitement and prosperity, attracting individuals from all walks of life. However, as the easily accessible gold deposits were depleted, the challenges of mining deep underground or in remote areas became more evident. Many miners struggled to find significant quantities of gold, and the dream of striking it rich proved elusive for most.

Despite the challenges and the eventual decline of the gold rushes, their legacy remains significant. The gold rush era played a crucial role in shaping the identity and character of Australia. It contributed to the growth of cities and towns, the development of mining technologies, and the establishment of democratic institutions.

The gold rush era also left an indelible mark on Australian culture and folklore. Stories of luck, perseverance, and resilience became woven into the national narrative, celebrated in literature, art, and music. The spirit of the gold rush era, with its sense of adventure and possibility, continues to resonate in the Australian psyche.

Reflecting on the gold rush era allows us to appreciate the complexities and nuances of this transformative period. It is a reminder of the highs and lows, the aspirations and challenges that shaped Australia's development.

# Bushrangers and Outlaws: Tales of Crime and Infamy

The era of bushrangers and outlaws in Australia's history conjures images of daring escapades, dangerous pursuits, and legendary figures whose exploits have become the stuff of folklore. This chapter delves into the tales of crime and infamy surrounding the bushrangers and outlaws who roamed the Australian wilderness during the 18th and 19th centuries.

Bushrangers were criminals who took to the bush, often escaping from convict settlements or rural areas, and evading the authorities as they engaged in acts of robbery, horse theft, and sometimes even murder. The harsh conditions of the Australian frontier, combined with the allure of adventure and the desire to escape the strictures of colonial society, fueled the rise of these outlaws.

One of the most notorious bushrangers was Ned Kelly, whose name has become synonymous with Australia's bushranging era. Born in 1854, Kelly's life and crimes captured the imagination of the public. His gang, which included his brother Dan Kelly and two associates, engaged in a series of brazen robberies and confrontations with the police. Their exploits and clashes with law enforcement culminated in the infamous siege at Glenrowan in 1880, where Ned Kelly donned his iconic suit of homemade armor. The Kelly Gang's story has become an enduring symbol of rebellion and defiance in Australian history.

Other prominent bushrangers include Ben Hall, Captain Thunderbolt (Frederick Ward), and Frank Gardiner, among many others. Each had their own unique stories, escapades, and interactions with the authorities. These bushrangers captured the public's attention and became folk heroes in some circles, while others saw them as dangerous criminals.

The bushrangers often operated in small groups, living in hideouts in the dense Australian bush. They would strike isolated homesteads, travelers, or coaches, demanding valuables and supplies. The bush provided cover and escape routes, making it difficult for the authorities to track them down. The romanticized image of the lone outlaw on horseback, evading capture and living by his own rules, has become deeply ingrained in Australian folklore.

While some bushrangers were opportunistic criminals, others were driven to a life of crime due to social and economic circumstances. Harsh living conditions, limited opportunities, and a sense of injustice in the face of inequality contributed to their choices. However, it is important to note that not all bushrangers were celebrated figures. Many innocent people fell victim to their crimes, and their actions caused fear and disruption within communities.

The authorities of the time, such as the police and armed forces, pursued bushrangers with determination. Rewards were offered for their capture, and extensive efforts were made to bring them to justice. The bushranging era sparked a heightened sense of law enforcement and measures to combat the activities of outlaws. The legend of the skilled bushranger-hunters, such as Captain Frederick Pottinger and Sergeant Michael Kennedy, who engaged in deadly encounters with bushrangers, further added to the folklore surrounding this period.

The bushranging era eventually came to an end as the colonies became more settled, communication and transportation networks improved, and law enforcement agencies became better equipped to deal with criminals. The rise of a more ordered society, along with changing attitudes and the establishment of legal systems, contributed to the decline of bushranging.

The legacy of the bushrangers and outlaws continues to captivate the public's imagination. Their tales of audacity, survival, and defiance against authority have been immortalized in literature, folk songs, and popular culture. The romanticized portrayal of the bushranger as a rebel against societal constraints reflects the fascination with those who dared to challenge the status quo.

It is essential to approach the stories of bushrangers and outlaws with a nuanced understanding of the historical context. While their deeds are often glorified, it is important to remember the real consequences of their actions and the impact on individuals and communities.

# Federation and the Birth of Modern Australia

The Federation of Australia, which took place on January 1, 1901, marks a significant milestone in the nation's history. It brought together the separate colonies of New South Wales, Victoria, Queensland, South Australia, Western Australia, and Tasmania, uniting them under a single federal government. The process of federation was a complex and deliberative journey that reflected the aspirations, challenges, and compromises of the time.

The movement towards federation gained momentum in the late 19th century, driven by various factors. Common concerns, such as defense, trade, and immigration, highlighted the need for greater coordination and cooperation between the colonies. The idea of a unified Australia appealed to many who sought a stronger national identity and a more efficient governance structure.

The road to federation was paved with discussions, conventions, and debates. In 1891, the first National Australasian Convention was held in Sydney, where delegates from the colonies gathered to discuss the principles and mechanisms of federation. This convention laid the groundwork for further negotiations and paved the way for subsequent meetings.

The second National Australasian Convention, held in Adelaide in 1897, resulted in the drafting of a constitution for the proposed federal government. The constitution outlined the division of powers between the federal and state governments, established a bicameral parliament, and set forth the framework for a range of legislative and executive functions.

The proposed constitution faced a series of hurdles before being accepted. It had to be ratified by the majority of voters in each colony, as well as receive approval from the British Parliament. Referendums were held in the colonies to seek public support for federation, and the constitution was eventually accepted by the required majority.

The passage of the Commonwealth of Australia Constitution Act by the British Parliament in 1900 paved the way for the formal establishment of the Australian Federation on January 1, 1901. The day is now celebrated as Australia Day, marking the birth of the modern nation.

The new federal government consisted of a Governor-General representing the British monarch, a Senate, and a House of Representatives. Edmund Barton became the first Prime Minister of Australia, leading a government responsible for matters of national significance, such as defense, foreign affairs, and trade.

Federation brought numerous benefits and challenges for the newly formed nation. It allowed for greater coordination in areas such as trade and defense, enabling Australia to negotiate as a single entity on the global stage. It also facilitated the development of a national identity and a sense of unity among the diverse population.

However, federation also posed challenges, particularly in reconciling the interests and powers of the federal and state governments. The balance of power and responsibilities between the two levels of government continues to be a subject of debate and refinement.

Federation represented a significant step towards self-governance and independence for Australia. While the nation remained part of the British Empire, it gained increased autonomy in matters of domestic policy and governance. Over time, Australia would further assert its independence, culminating in the Australia Act of 1986, which severed the last vestiges of legal ties with the British Parliament.

The legacy of federation continues to shape modern Australia. It forms the basis of the country's political system, fostering a democratic and representative form of government. The principles enshrined in the constitution, such as the division of powers and the protection of individual rights, continue to guide the nation's legal and political landscape.

Federation also reflects Australia's ongoing journey towards inclusivity and recognition of its Indigenous peoples. The preamble to the constitution recognizes the prior occupation of Australia by Aboriginal and Torres Strait Islander peoples and acknowledges their continuing cultures, languages, and traditions.

The process of federation was a significant chapter in Australia's history, marking the birth of a modern nation. It symbolizes the aspirations, compromises, and collective efforts of the Australian people to forge a unified country. Reflecting on this pivotal period offers valuable insights into the nation's democratic foundations, the complexities of governance, and the ongoing pursuit of a harmonious and inclusive society.

# World War I: Australia's Sacrifice and Nationhood

World War I, which took place from 1914 to 1918, had a profound impact on Australia and played a significant role in shaping the nation's identity. The war was a global conflict that involved many countries, and Australia's involvement demonstrated its commitment to the British Empire, as well as its growing sense of nationhood.

When Britain declared war on Germany in August 1914, Australia, as a member of the British Empire, pledged its support. The nation's response was marked by a wave of patriotism and a sense of duty to the Empire. Thousands of young Australian men volunteered to serve in the armed forces, driven by a desire to defend their homeland and contribute to the war effort.

The Australian Imperial Force (AIF) was formed to represent Australia in the war. The AIF consisted of infantry, cavalry, artillery, engineers, and support units. The first contingent of Australian troops, numbering over 20,000, set sail for Egypt in October 1914, where they would undergo training before being deployed to the Western Front.

The Gallipoli Campaign, which commenced in April 1915, became a defining moment in Australia's involvement in the war. The aim of the campaign was to capture the Gallipoli Peninsula in modern-day Turkey and open a new front against the Central Powers. However, the campaign resulted in heavy casualties and protracted stalemate. Australian and New Zealand troops, known as the Anzacs

(Australian and New Zealand Army Corps), demonstrated resilience and bravery during the grueling and costly campaign.

While the Gallipoli Campaign ended in evacuation in December 1915, the Anzac legend was born. The bravery and endurance displayed by the Australian soldiers at Gallipoli became an enduring symbol of Australian identity and the values of mateship, courage, and determination. Anzac Day, commemorated on April 25 each year, honors the sacrifice of all Australian and New Zealand service personnel in subsequent wars as well.

The majority of Australian troops were subsequently deployed to the Western Front in Europe. They fought alongside British, Canadian, and other Allied forces in battles such as the Somme, Ypres, and Passchendaele. The conditions on the Western Front were incredibly challenging, with trenches, mud, and constant exposure to enemy fire.

The toll on Australian soldiers was significant. Over 60,000 Australians lost their lives during the war, and many more were injured or suffered long-lasting physical and psychological trauma. The war had a profound impact on families and communities across the country, with nearly every Australian town and city touched by loss and grief.

Australia's participation in World War I also contributed to a growing sense of nationhood and an increased desire for recognition as an independent nation on the world stage. The sacrifices made by Australian troops, coupled with the experiences of those at home who supported the war effort, fostered a sense of unity and pride in the nation's contribution.

The war also had far-reaching social and economic effects. The mobilization of Australian industry to support the war effort led to increased manufacturing and production. Women played an important role on the home front, taking on jobs traditionally held by men and contributing to the war effort in various capacities.

World War I marked a significant turning point in Australia's history. The sacrifices made during the war and the sense of nationhood that emerged from the conflict set the stage for Australia's increasing independence and its evolving position within the British Empire.

The aftermath of the war brought changes to the political landscape of Australia as well. The experiences of the war, combined with other social and political factors, led to the emergence of new ideas and movements. This included the rise of the Australian Labor Party, which championed the rights of workers and played a significant role in shaping the future of Australian politics.

The legacy of World War I is deeply embedded in Australia's collective memory and national identity. The war's impact on the nation's psyche, its contribution to the Anzac spirit, and the sacrifices made by Australian soldiers continue to be commemorated and honored to this day.

# The Roaring Twenties: Social Change and Economic Growth

The 1920s, often referred to as the Roaring Twenties or the Jazz Age, was a decade of significant social change and economic growth in many parts of the world, including Australia. This chapter explores the transformative aspects of this period and their impact on Australian society.

Following the end of World War I, Australia experienced a period of relative prosperity and optimism. The war had brought economic opportunities and increased demand for Australian goods and resources. The return of soldiers from the war, combined with the easing of government controls, led to a surge in economic activity and a sense of liberation.

One of the defining features of the Roaring Twenties was the emergence of a vibrant and cosmopolitan urban culture. Cities like Sydney and Melbourne experienced rapid growth and became hubs of social and cultural activity. The advent of modern transportation, such as automobiles and trams, made it easier for people to travel and connect with one another.

The 1920s witnessed a boom in entertainment and leisure activities. Jazz music, which originated in the United States, became popular in Australia, particularly among the younger generation. Dance halls, jazz clubs, and speakeasies proliferated, offering opportunities for socializing and indulging in the latest trends.

Flapper culture, characterized by women challenging traditional gender norms through fashion, behavior, and a newfound sense of independence, emerged during this period. Flappers were known for their short haircuts, shorter skirts, and rejection of conventional Victorian-era ideals. They symbolized a growing spirit of freedom and female empowerment.

The economic growth of the 1920s was fueled by a variety of factors. Australia experienced a surge in manufacturing and industrial production, leading to job creation and increased consumer spending. The country's agricultural sector also thrived, with wheat, wool, and other commodities in high demand both domestically and internationally.

The availability of consumer goods expanded, as did purchasing power. Australians embraced new technologies and products, such as radios, refrigerators, and electric appliances. This era witnessed a shift towards a more consumer-driven society, with advertising playing a significant role in promoting the allure of modernity and the acquisition of material possessions.

The prosperity of the 1920s was not shared equally among all Australians. While urban areas experienced growth and affluence, rural communities faced challenges, including falling agricultural prices and droughts. Indigenous Australians and some minority groups faced discrimination and limited access to opportunities.

The 1920s also saw advancements in women's rights and political participation. In 1922, Edith Cowan became the first woman elected to an Australian parliament. Women's suffrage expanded, granting voting rights to more women across the country. The decade marked progress in the fight for gender equality, although significant barriers and inequalities persisted.

However, the economic boom of the 1920s was not sustainable. Towards the end of the decade, signs of economic instability began to emerge. The global financial crisis of 1929, also known as the Great Depression, had a severe impact on Australia's economy. The subsequent years would bring economic hardship and social upheaval.

The Roaring Twenties represented a unique period of social and cultural transformation in Australia. The decade witnessed increased urbanization, changing gender roles, and a consumer-driven society. The era symbolized a sense of optimism, modernity, and an embrace of new possibilities.

The legacy of the Roaring Twenties is still felt in contemporary Australian society. The advancements in women's rights, the cultural shifts, and the enduring influence of the jazz age on music and entertainment have left a lasting impact. Reflecting on this era allows us to appreciate the dynamism and complexities of Australia's past and the ongoing process of societal evolution.

# The Great Depression: Hardship and Resilience

The Great Depression, which began with the stock market crash in 1929 and lasted throughout much of the 1930s, was a period of profound economic and social hardship worldwide, including Australia. This chapter explores the impact of the Great Depression on the country and the resilience demonstrated by its people in the face of adversity.

The effects of the global economic downturn reached Australia swiftly. The country's heavy reliance on exports, particularly agricultural and mining products, made it highly vulnerable to the decline in international trade. The crash of the stock market in 1929 triggered a sharp decline in commodity prices, leading to a severe contraction in the Australian economy.

The consequences of the Great Depression were far-reaching. Mass unemployment became a pervasive problem as businesses closed down or scaled back operations. Unemployment rates soared, peaking at over 30% in some areas. Many Australians struggled to find work and provide for their families, leading to significant economic and social upheaval.

The agricultural sector, which had been a pillar of the Australian economy, was hit particularly hard. Falling prices, droughts, and reduced demand for agricultural products resulted in financial ruin for many farmers. The rural communities, already grappling with the challenges of the 1920s, faced even greater hardships during the Great Depression.

Urban areas were also deeply affected by the economic crisis. Poverty and homelessness became more prevalent, with families living in makeshift dwellings known as "tent cities" or seeking refuge in overcrowded slums. The lack of social safety nets meant that many Australians faced destitution and relied on charitable assistance to survive.

The government's response to the Great Depression varied over time. Initially, the government relied on orthodox economic policies of austerity and balanced budgets. However, as the severity of the crisis became apparent, the government began to implement measures aimed at providing relief and stimulating the economy.

In 1931, the newly elected Prime Minister, James Scullin, introduced the Premiers' Plan, a scheme designed to reduce government spending and balance the budget. However, the plan faced opposition and was criticized for exacerbating the economic downturn. It was eventually abandoned, and a new approach emphasizing public works and increased government spending gained traction.

The government's response also included the establishment of the Commonwealth Bank in 1932, which aimed to stabilize the banking system and provide credit to struggling industries. The bank played a significant role in supporting the economy and assisting individuals and businesses during the crisis.

The Great Depression had a profound impact on Australian society. It tested the resilience of individuals, families, and communities. Mutual support and solidarity became crucial for survival. Local organizations, charities, and community groups mobilized to provide assistance, including food, clothing, and shelter to those in need.

The artistic and cultural landscape of the country was also influenced by the Great Depression. Artists, writers, and musicians reflected the prevailing mood of hardship and despair in their work. The social commentary and critiques of economic inequality expressed during this time continue to resonate in the collective memory of Australia's cultural heritage.

The resilience and resourcefulness of the Australian people during the Great Depression were remarkable. Individuals sought alternative ways to make a living, including taking on odd jobs, bartering, or establishing small-scale enterprises. Families and communities supported one another, sharing resources and providing emotional support in times of distress.

The end of the Great Depression in Australia came gradually with the onset of World War II in the late 1930s. The demand for resources and production for war efforts provided a boost to the economy and led to a gradual recovery. However, the scars of the Great Depression would continue to shape Australian society for years to come.

The legacy of the Great Depression is one of hardship, resilience, and the importance of social safety nets. The experience served as a reminder of the need for economic stability, government intervention during times of crisis, and the importance of fostering a sense of community and support for those facing adversity.

# World War II: Australia on the Frontline

World War II, which spanned from 1939 to 1945, had a profound impact on Australia and its position in the global conflict. This chapter explores Australia's involvement in the war, the challenges faced on the home front, and the nation's contributions to the Allied victory.

Australia's entry into World War II was prompted by the outbreak of war in Europe and the growing threat posed by the Axis powers, particularly Japan. The nation's security and strategic interests were closely tied to its alliances, particularly with the United Kingdom and the United States.

The war in the Pacific became a major focus for Australia's military efforts. The bombing of Darwin by Japanese forces in 1942 signaled the vulnerability of the Australian mainland and heightened fears of invasion. The threat of Japanese expansion in the region and the subsequent battles, such as the Kokoda Track campaign and the Battle of the Coral Sea, brought the war directly to Australia's doorstep.

The Australian military, known as the Australian Imperial Force (AIF), played a significant role in the war effort. Australian troops fought alongside Allied forces in campaigns across the Pacific, the Middle East, and Europe. The defense of Australian territories, such as New Guinea, Papua, and the islands of the Pacific, became critical in resisting Japanese advances.

The home front in Australia was transformed by the demands of war. The nation mobilized its resources and industries to support the war effort. Factories were repurposed for wartime production, and the manufacturing sector shifted its focus to the production of military equipment and supplies. Women entered the workforce in larger numbers, taking on roles traditionally held by men who had enlisted in the military.

Rationing and scarcity became a way of life during the war. Essential goods, such as food, clothing, and fuel, were subject to strict rationing measures to ensure equitable distribution. Australians were encouraged to support the war effort through voluntary organizations, such as the Australian Comforts Fund, which provided care packages and support to servicemen overseas.

The Australian population faced the challenges of wartime restrictions and the constant threat of enemy attacks. Air raid drills and blackouts were implemented to protect against potential bombings. Civil defense organizations were established to maintain public safety and coordinate emergency responses.

The impact of the war was felt deeply by Australian families and communities. Many servicemen and women left their homes to serve abroad, often facing dangerous and life-threatening situations. The loss of loved ones, as well as the physical and emotional toll of war, left lasting scars on the nation.

Australia's involvement in World War II was not limited to the military sphere. The country also played a significant role in intelligence operations and diplomatic efforts. Australian codebreakers at the Central Bureau in

Melbourne contributed to crucial intelligence breakthroughs, particularly in the Pacific theater. Australian politicians and diplomats participated in conferences and negotiations that shaped the post-war order, such as the establishment of the United Nations.

The end of World War II brought both relief and challenges for Australia. The nation celebrated the Allied victory and the return of its servicemen and women. However, the war had fundamentally altered the global landscape, and Australia faced the task of rebuilding and adjusting to a new world order.

The legacy of World War II continues to shape Australia's national identity. The experiences of the war, the sacrifices made by its citizens, and the enduring bonds with Allied nations left a profound impact on the nation's collective memory. Commemorations such as Anzac Day and Remembrance Day serve as reminders of the price paid for freedom and the ongoing duty to honor those who served.

# Post-War Reconstruction: A Nation Rebuilds

The aftermath of World War II brought both challenges and opportunities for Australia as it embarked on the task of post-war reconstruction. This chapter explores the efforts made to rebuild the nation, reshape its economy, and address the social and political changes that followed the war.

In the immediate post-war period, Australia faced the task of demobilizing its military forces and reintegrating returning servicemen and women into civilian life. The repatriation process involved providing support for veterans, including housing, employment, and healthcare services. The Returned Services League (RSL) played a significant role in advocating for the rights and welfare of returned soldiers.

Economically, the post-war years were characterized by a shift from wartime production to peacetime industries. The manufacturing sector diversified, focusing on consumer goods and infrastructure development. The Snowy Mountains Scheme, a large-scale hydroelectric and irrigation project, became a symbol of Australia's post-war reconstruction efforts, providing employment opportunities and fostering technological advancements.

The war had left an indelible impact on the Australian economy. The country's industrial capacity and infrastructure were strained by the demands of war, and rebuilding was necessary. The government implemented various measures to stimulate economic growth, including investment in public infrastructure projects, subsidies for industries, and the expansion of social welfare programs.

Migration also played a significant role in Australia's post-war reconstruction. The government initiated various immigration schemes to attract skilled workers and address labor shortages. The first large-scale migration program, known as the "Populate or Perish" policy, aimed to increase Australia's population and foster economic growth. As a result, waves of migrants from Europe, including displaced persons and war refugees, arrived in Australia, enriching the country's cultural diversity.

The changing demographic landscape and the influx of migrants had a profound impact on Australian society. It brought new customs, languages, and traditions, transforming the cultural fabric of the nation. However, it also led to debates and challenges surrounding issues of integration, multiculturalism, and identity.

The post-war years saw significant social and political changes. The experiences of war and the growing demand for social justice fueled movements for equality and reforms. Women's rights, indigenous rights, and workers' rights were prominent issues that gained traction during this period. The 1967 referendum, which granted full citizenship rights to Aboriginal and Torres Strait Islander peoples, was a significant milestone in addressing historical injustices.

The political landscape of Australia also underwent significant transformation. The Australian Labor Party, with its platform of social democracy and welfare reforms, gained prominence and implemented policies aimed at creating a more equitable society. The Liberal Party, on the other hand, emphasized free-market principles and supported economic liberalization.

Australia's post-war reconstruction efforts were not without challenges. The process of transitioning from a war economy to a peacetime economy brought about inflation, housing shortages, and industrial disputes. However, the nation's resilience and determination to rebuild prevailed.

The reconstruction period also marked a shift in Australia's international relations. The nation sought to assert its independence and autonomy, leading to a reevaluation of its traditional ties with the United Kingdom. Australia played an active role in the formation of international organizations, such as the United Nations, and participated in peacekeeping missions and humanitarian efforts around the world.

The legacy of Australia's post-war reconstruction is evident in the nation's modern landscape. The infrastructure projects, industrial diversification, and social reforms implemented during this period laid the foundation for Australia's continued growth and development. The social progress achieved, such as advancements in healthcare, education, and workers' rights, contributed to the creation of a more inclusive and prosperous society.

Reflecting on the post-war reconstruction era allows us to appreciate the resilience and adaptability of the Australian people. It is a testament to their ability to overcome adversity and rebuild a nation, fostering a sense of national identity and pride in the achievements of the post-war generation.

The task of post-war reconstruction was a complex and multifaceted undertaking, encompassing economic, social, and political dimensions. The efforts made during this period shaped the Australia we know today, embodying the spirit of progress, innovation, and the pursuit of a better future for all Australians.

# The Snowy Mountains Scheme: Engineering Marvel of the South

The Snowy Mountains Scheme stands as one of Australia's most ambitious and remarkable engineering projects. Spanning over 25 years from its commencement in 1949, the scheme aimed to harness the power of the Snowy River and its tributaries to generate hydroelectricity and provide irrigation for agricultural development. This chapter delves into the intricacies of the scheme, highlighting its significance and lasting impact.

The idea for the Snowy Mountains Scheme originated in the early 20th century, with initial surveys and investigations conducted to assess the feasibility of such an undertaking. The region's abundant water resources, high elevation, and mountainous terrain presented an opportunity to tap into the potential of hydroelectric power and water management.

The scheme involved the construction of a series of dams, tunnels, aqueducts, power stations, and reservoirs. It required extensive planning, engineering expertise, and a massive workforce to execute the complex network of infrastructure. The Australian government, recognizing the potential benefits, committed to the project as a cornerstone of the nation's post-war reconstruction efforts.

The Snowy Mountains Scheme relied on a multicultural and multinational workforce. Immigrants, including engineers, laborers, and tradespeople from over 30 countries, flocked to the region, bringing with them their skills, knowledge, and cultural diversity. This multicultural collaboration fostered a sense of camaraderie and unity among the workers, leaving a lasting legacy in Australian society.

The construction of the Snowy Mountains Scheme was a monumental undertaking, characterized by its scale and technical complexity. The scheme involved diverting water from the Snowy River and its tributaries through an intricate system of tunnels, aqueducts, and canals. These waterways facilitated the transfer of water to power stations and irrigation areas, spanning across New South Wales and Victoria.

The hydroelectric power generated by the Snowy Mountains Scheme played a crucial role in meeting Australia's energy needs. The scheme's seven power stations, including the iconic Tumut 3 Power Station, produced a substantial amount of electricity, providing a reliable and renewable energy source for homes, industries, and infrastructure development.

The Snowy Mountains Scheme also revolutionized agricultural practices in the region. The diverted water was used to irrigate vast areas of farmland, facilitating the cultivation of crops and enabling agricultural diversification. The increased water supply transformed arid landscapes into fertile agricultural areas, boosting productivity and supporting rural communities.

Beyond its engineering and economic significance, the Snowy Mountains Scheme had a profound environmental impact. The introduction of regulated water flow and irrigation systems allowed for improved water management, leading to ecological restoration and habitat creation for native flora and fauna. Efforts were made to mitigate the environmental impact of the scheme and preserve the unique ecosystem of the Snowy Mountains region.

The completion of the Snowy Mountains Scheme in 1974 marked a monumental achievement in Australian engineering history. The scheme not only realized its goals of hydroelectricity generation and irrigation but also exemplified the nation's ability to undertake and deliver large-scale infrastructure projects. It showcased Australian innovation, ingenuity, and technical expertise on the global stage.

The Snowy Mountains Scheme continues to play a crucial role in Australia's energy landscape. It remains an integral part of the country's power generation infrastructure, providing clean and renewable energy to meet the growing demands of a modern society. The scheme's legacy extends beyond its immediate benefits, standing as a symbol of Australia's engineering prowess and the enduring spirit of nation-building.

The Snowy Mountains Scheme is celebrated as an iconic achievement in Australian history. It represents the collaborative efforts of thousands of workers, engineers, and visionaries who overcame significant challenges to realize a project of unprecedented scale and complexity. The scheme's enduring legacy serves as a reminder of Australia's ability to harness its natural resources, drive innovation, and shape its future through bold and ambitious endeavors.

# The Stolen Generations: Dark Chapter in Australia's History

The Stolen Generations represent one of the darkest chapters in Australia's history, marking a period of profound pain, loss, and trauma for Indigenous Australians. This chapter delves into the policies and practices that led to the forced removal of Indigenous children from their families, the impact it had on individuals and communities, and the ongoing process of reconciliation.

The Stolen Generations refers to a period spanning several decades, from approximately the late 1800s to the 1970s, during which Indigenous children were forcibly removed from their families and communities by government authorities. These removals were carried out under various policies and legislation implemented by federal, state, and territory governments.

The motivations behind the forced removals were multifaceted. The prevailing ideology at the time was one of assimilation, with the belief that removing Indigenous children from their families and cultural roots would facilitate their integration into white society. Authorities justified these actions by claiming they were acting in the best interests of the children, aiming to provide them with education, healthcare, and opportunities for a "better" life.

The removals occurred across Australia, affecting Indigenous communities in urban, rural, and remote areas. Children were taken from their families, often without consent or adequate explanation, and placed in institutions, missions, foster homes, or adopted by non-Indigenous families. The separation from their families, culture, and language had devastating consequences for the individuals involved and their communities.

The impact of the Stolen Generations on Indigenous individuals and families cannot be overstated. The forced removals resulted in the loss of cultural identity, connection to country, language, and traditional knowledge. The trauma experienced by those who were taken, as well as the intergenerational trauma passed down through subsequent generations, continues to reverberate within Indigenous communities.

The effects of the Stolen Generations are wide-ranging and complex. Many individuals experienced physical and emotional abuse in institutions and foster homes, further compounding their trauma. The loss of family connections and cultural heritage led to a profound sense of dislocation, grief, and a fractured sense of identity for those affected.

In the years following the recognition of the Stolen Generations, numerous inquiries, commissions, and court cases were initiated to investigate and address the injustices inflicted upon Indigenous Australians. The Bringing Them Home report, released in 1997 as a result of the National Inquiry into the Separation of Aboriginal and Torres Strait Islander Children from Their Families, provided significant insights into the extent and impacts of the removals.

The Australian government, along with state and territory governments, has formally acknowledged and apologized for the policies and practices that led to the Stolen Generations. The national apology, delivered by then-Prime Minister Kevin Rudd in 2008, sought to acknowledge the past wrongs, express remorse, and commit to a process of healing, reconciliation, and addressing the ongoing effects of the forced removals.

Reconciliation between Indigenous and non-Indigenous Australians remains an ongoing process. Efforts have been made to promote truth-telling, support healing, and foster greater understanding and respect for Indigenous culture and rights. Initiatives such as the establishment of the National Sorry Day and the Reconciliation Action Plan framework aim to promote dialogue, understanding, and meaningful change.

The Stolen Generations represent a significant stain on Australia's history, highlighting the systemic discrimination and mistreatment of Indigenous peoples. Acknowledging this dark chapter is crucial in understanding the ongoing impact of colonization and the importance of addressing historical injustices.

# Indigenous Rights and Reconciliation: The Road to Healing

The struggle for Indigenous rights and reconciliation in Australia represents a significant milestone in the nation's history. This chapter explores the journey towards acknowledging and respecting the rights of Indigenous Australians, the pursuit of reconciliation, and the ongoing efforts to heal the wounds of the past.

Indigenous rights have been a key focus of advocacy and activism in Australia for many decades. The 1967 referendum, which saw an overwhelming majority of Australians vote in favor of amending the Constitution to include Indigenous Australians in the national census and grant the federal government power to legislate on their behalf, marked a pivotal moment in recognizing the need for change.

Following the referendum, efforts were made to address the injustices inflicted upon Indigenous Australians and to secure their rights. Land rights and native title became significant areas of focus, with landmark legal cases such as the Mabo decision in 1992 and the Native Title Act of 1993 leading to increased recognition of Indigenous land rights and ownership.

The pursuit of reconciliation, a process aimed at healing the relationship between Indigenous and non-Indigenous Australians, gained momentum in the late 20th century. The Council for Aboriginal Reconciliation, established in 1991, played a vital role in fostering dialogue, understanding, and building relationships between Indigenous and non-Indigenous Australians.

In 2000, the Council for Aboriginal Reconciliation presented its final report, "Reconciliation: Australia's Challenge." This report called for a range of actions, including the recognition of Indigenous peoples in the Constitution, addressing historical injustices, promoting cultural diversity, and supporting self-determination for Indigenous communities.

The apology delivered by then-Prime Minister Kevin Rudd in 2008 was a significant milestone in the journey towards reconciliation. The national apology sought to acknowledge the pain and suffering inflicted upon Indigenous Australians, express remorse for past wrongs, and commit to a path of healing and understanding.

The process of reconciliation extends beyond symbolic gestures. It encompasses efforts to address the socio-economic disparities faced by Indigenous communities, promote cultural preservation, and empower Indigenous Australians in decision-making processes that affect their lives and lands. Programs such as the Closing the Gap initiative aim to reduce the gaps in health, education, employment, and life expectancy between Indigenous and non-Indigenous Australians.

Collaboration and partnership between Indigenous and non-Indigenous Australians are essential for the successful pursuit of reconciliation. Reconciliation Action Plans (RAPs) have been developed by various organizations, including government agencies, businesses, and educational institutions, as a framework for promoting reconciliation through practical actions and commitments.

Indigenous voices and perspectives are increasingly being amplified and respected in all facets of Australian society. Indigenous art, music, literature, and storytelling play a vital role in preserving cultural heritage and fostering understanding. Indigenous knowledge systems and practices are recognized for their unique contributions to sustainable land management, environmental conservation, and holistic approaches to well-being.

The path to healing and reconciliation is complex and multifaceted. It requires ongoing commitment, education, and reflection from all Australians. Truth-telling and acknowledging the historical injustices and ongoing challenges faced by Indigenous Australians are fundamental to the process.

The journey towards healing and reconciliation is not without its challenges. The legacy of colonization, dispossession, and systemic discrimination continues to impact Indigenous communities. Disparities in health, education, employment, and social outcomes persist, requiring sustained efforts to address structural inequalities.

However, the progress made in recent decades demonstrates a growing recognition of the importance of Indigenous rights, self-determination, and reconciliation. The establishment of the Uluru Statement from the Heart in 2017, calling for constitutional recognition and a First Nations voice in parliament, represents a significant milestone in Indigenous-led advocacy and the quest for meaningful change.

Reflecting on the road to healing and reconciliation allows us to appreciate the resilience, strength, and cultural richness of Indigenous Australians. It reminds us of the ongoing responsibility to actively support and promote Indigenous rights, foster respectful relationships, and work towards a just and inclusive society for all Australians. The journey towards reconciliation is a collective endeavor that requires ongoing commitment, empathy, and a willingness to confront the challenges of the past while striving for a shared future.

# From White Australia to Multiculturalism: Immigration and Identity

The transformation of Australia from a predominantly homogeneous society under the policy of White Australia to a multicultural nation has shaped the country's identity and enriched its cultural fabric. This chapter explores the history of immigration in Australia, the evolution of immigration policies, and the impact on the nation's identity.

Australia's immigration history can be traced back to the arrival of the First Fleet in 1788, which brought British convicts and settlers to the continent. In the following decades, immigration predominantly consisted of individuals from the United Kingdom and Ireland, contributing to the establishment of a British-oriented society.

The policy of White Australia, implemented in the late 19th and early 20th centuries, aimed to restrict non-European immigration and maintain a predominantly Anglo-Celtic population. The policy was rooted in notions of racial superiority, fears of economic competition, and concerns about maintaining cultural and social homogeneity.

In the years following World War II, Australia witnessed a shift in its immigration policies and attitudes. The devastation of the war, coupled with the need for population growth and economic development, prompted the government to reassess its approach to immigration.

The abolition of the White Australia Policy in the late 1960s marked a significant turning point.

The post-war period saw an influx of migrants from diverse backgrounds, including Southern Europeans, Eastern Europeans, and Asians. These new arrivals brought with them their languages, traditions, and cultural practices, enriching the social fabric of Australian society. The government actively encouraged migration through various programs, such as the Ten Pound Poms initiative, which aimed to attract British migrants.

The changing demographics and increased cultural diversity of Australia prompted a shift in national identity and the emergence of multiculturalism as an official policy. The 1970s saw the introduction of multiculturalism as a guiding principle, recognizing the value of cultural diversity and promoting equality and respect for all Australians, regardless of their cultural backgrounds.

Multiculturalism in Australia encompasses a range of policies and practices aimed at fostering social cohesion, promoting cultural exchange, and supporting the rights and contributions of individuals from diverse backgrounds. It acknowledges the rights of individuals to maintain their cultural heritage while actively participating in the broader Australian society.

The impact of multiculturalism is evident in various aspects of Australian society. Cuisine, language, art, music, and literature have all been influenced by the cultural diversity of the nation. Festivals, celebrations, and community events showcase the richness of different cultures, creating opportunities for cross-cultural interactions and understanding.

The process of multiculturalism has not been without challenges. Issues of social cohesion, discrimination, and inequality persist in certain pockets of Australian society. However, efforts are being made to address these challenges through education, community engagement, and policies that promote equality and inclusivity.

Australia's immigration policies continue to evolve to meet the changing needs and circumstances of the nation. Skilled migration, family reunification, and refugee resettlement programs form part of the current immigration framework. Striking a balance between maintaining border security, meeting labor market demands, and upholding humanitarian values remains an ongoing challenge.

The future of immigration and identity in Australia is likely to be shaped by global trends, economic factors, and societal dynamics. The recognition of Indigenous rights and the increasing emphasis on reconciliation also play a significant role in shaping Australia's identity as a multicultural nation.

Reflecting on the journey from White Australia to multiculturalism allows us to appreciate the transformative power of immigration and cultural diversity. It highlights the importance of embracing pluralism, promoting social inclusion, and recognizing the contributions of individuals from diverse backgrounds.

The story of immigration in Australia is an ongoing narrative, intertwined with the nation's history and aspirations for a just and harmonious society. It is a testament to the adaptability and resilience of Australians, as well as a celebration of the multicultural tapestry that continues to define the country's identity.

# Mateship and the Anzac Spirit: Australia's Military Legacy

Australia's military legacy is deeply rooted in the values of mateship and the Anzac spirit. This chapter explores the significance of these ideals, their origins in Australia's military history, and their enduring impact on the nation's identity.

Mateship, a term commonly used in Australia, refers to a strong sense of loyalty, camaraderie, and mutual support among friends and colleagues. It has long been regarded as a defining characteristic of Australian culture, and its roots can be traced back to the experiences of Australian soldiers during times of conflict.

The Anzac spirit, derived from the acronym ANZAC (Australian and New Zealand Army Corps), symbolizes the qualities of courage, resilience, and sacrifice exhibited by Australian and New Zealand troops during World War I. The Anzacs, particularly those who fought at Gallipoli in 1915, have become central figures in Australia's military history and collective memory.

The concept of mateship and the Anzac spirit emerged in the crucible of war. Australian soldiers, many of whom were volunteers, formed close bonds with their comrades as they faced the hardships, dangers, and horrors of battle. In the face of adversity, they relied on each other for support, forging a strong sense of trust and unity.

The Gallipoli campaign, a significant chapter in Australia's military history, played a pivotal role in shaping the Anzac spirit. The campaign, launched as an attempt to secure the Dardanelles and open a new front against the Central Powers, resulted in heavy casualties for the Anzac forces. Despite the military failure, the courage, determination, and unwavering loyalty displayed by the Anzacs became emblematic of the Australian fighting spirit.

The Anzac spirit extends beyond Gallipoli and World War I. It encompasses the contributions and sacrifices made by Australian servicemen and women in subsequent conflicts, including World War II, the Korean War, the Vietnam War, and modern peacekeeping missions. The qualities of courage, selflessness, and mateship continue to be revered and celebrated within the Australian military community.

Anzac Day, observed on April 25th each year, holds great significance in Australia. It commemorates the landing at Gallipoli and serves as a day of remembrance for all Australians who have served and died in war or on peacekeeping operations. Dawn services, marches, and solemn ceremonies are held across the country to honor the Anzac legacy and pay tribute to those who have made the ultimate sacrifice.

The ideals of mateship and the Anzac spirit resonate beyond the military context. They have become part of the broader Australian identity, representing values that extend to everyday life. Mateship is celebrated as a spirit of solidarity, egalitarianism, and support for one another, fostering a strong sense of community and resilience.

The Anzac spirit also underscores Australia's commitment to international alliances and cooperation. It has forged enduring bonds between Australia and New Zealand, as well as with other nations who have shared in the Anzac experience. The Anzac spirit serves as a reminder of the importance of collective efforts, mutual respect, and unity in the pursuit of peace and security.

While mateship and the Anzac spirit are deeply ingrained in Australian culture, it is important to recognize that they are not without their complexities. The idealization of the Anzac legend can sometimes overshadow the diverse experiences and perspectives of individuals within the military community. It is essential to foster a nuanced understanding of Australia's military legacy and to support the well-being and welfare of veterans and their families.

The enduring significance of mateship and the Anzac spirit lies in their ability to inspire and unite Australians across generations. They serve as a reminder of the sacrifices made by those who have served in the defense of the nation and the values of loyalty, resilience, and solidarity that underpin the Australian character.

As Australia continues to honor its military legacy, it is crucial to uphold the welfare and support of current and former servicemen and women. This includes recognizing the diverse experiences and needs within the military community and providing the necessary resources and services for their well-being.

Mateship and the Anzac spirit remain cornerstones of Australia's military heritage and national identity. They reflect the unwavering bonds formed in times of adversity and the shared commitment to serving the nation. The ideals of mateship and the Anzac spirit will continue to shape the collective conscience of the Australian people and serve as a reminder of the sacrifices and values that define the nation's military legacy.

# Women's Suffrage and the Fight for Equality

The struggle for women's suffrage and gender equality has been a defining chapter in Australia's history. This chapter explores the efforts and achievements of women in their fight for the right to vote and broader equality, highlighting the milestones, challenges, and ongoing quest for gender parity.

In the late 19th and early 20th centuries, women in Australia began to organize and advocate for their right to participate in the democratic process. Inspired by international suffrage movements and motivated by a desire for equal rights and representation, Australian women embarked on a journey towards suffrage.

South Australia led the way in 1894 by becoming the first Australian colony to grant women the right to vote in parliamentary elections. This breakthrough was followed by other colonies, with Western Australia (1899), New South Wales (1902), Tasmania (1903), Queensland (1905), and Victoria (1908) gradually extending suffrage to women.

The federal government, established in 1901 with the formation of the Commonwealth of Australia, initially excluded women from voting in federal elections. However, in 1902, the Commonwealth Franchise Act was passed, granting white women over the age of 21 the right to vote and stand for election to the federal parliament.

The suffrage movement in Australia was marked by the tireless efforts of many courageous and determined women. Leaders such as Vida Goldstein, Catherine Helen Spence, and Mary Lee played significant roles in advocating for women's rights and challenging the prevailing societal norms.

The suffrage campaign faced numerous challenges and opposition. Women encountered resistance from those who believed that their place was solely within the domestic sphere and that they lacked the capability to engage in political affairs. Anti-suffrage sentiment, rooted in gender stereotypes and entrenched biases, posed obstacles to achieving voting rights.

Women's suffrage was not the only goal of the movement. It was part of a broader fight for gender equality, encompassing issues such as property rights, legal recognition, access to education and employment, and the elimination of discriminatory practices.

The achievement of suffrage marked a significant turning point, empowering women to actively participate in the democratic process and shape the political landscape of Australia. Women began to stand for election, with Edith Cowan becoming the first woman elected to an Australian parliament in 1921.

The suffrage movement laid the foundation for subsequent advancements in women's rights. In the decades that followed, women in Australia continued to challenge gender norms and work towards greater equality. The 1960s and 1970s witnessed the emergence of the second-wave feminist movement, which addressed issues such as reproductive rights, workplace discrimination, and gender-based violence.

Legislation was introduced to address gender inequality and discrimination. The Sex Discrimination Act of 1984 and subsequent reforms aimed to prohibit discrimination on the basis of sex, pregnancy, marital status, and family responsibilities. These measures provided a legal framework to protect women's rights and promote gender equality.

Despite significant progress, challenges and inequities persist. Women continue to face gender-based discrimination, underrepresentation in leadership positions, and wage disparities. Intersectional factors such as race, ethnicity, and socioeconomic status further compound these inequalities, highlighting the need for ongoing efforts to achieve true gender equality.

The fight for gender equality extends beyond legal rights and representation. It encompasses broader cultural and societal changes, challenging ingrained biases, and promoting gender-inclusive practices. Education, awareness, and the dismantling of gender stereotypes are critical in fostering a more equitable and inclusive society.

Women's suffrage and the ongoing struggle for gender equality have shaped Australia's social, political, and cultural landscape. They represent the tireless efforts of individuals and movements that have challenged the status quo, expanded opportunities for women, and advanced the principles of equality and justice.

# Indigenous Land Rights: Struggles and Achievements

The recognition and restoration of Indigenous land rights in Australia have been at the forefront of the ongoing struggle for justice, self-determination, and reconciliation. This chapter explores the historical struggles, significant achievements, and ongoing challenges faced by Indigenous Australians in their pursuit of land rights.

The dispossession of Indigenous lands began with the arrival of European settlers in 1788. The British colonizers asserted sovereignty over the continent, disregarding the longstanding connection of Indigenous peoples to their ancestral lands. The ensuing frontier conflicts, forced removals, and discriminatory policies further marginalized and dispossessed Indigenous communities of their traditional lands.

For many years, Indigenous peoples faced enormous obstacles in reclaiming their land rights. The legal system and governmental policies were largely skewed against them, denying their inherent rights and dismissing their claims to their ancestral territories. This systemic injustice perpetuated a cycle of dispossession and erasure of Indigenous cultural heritage.

The fight for Indigenous land rights gained momentum in the 20th century, driven by the resilience, activism, and advocacy of Indigenous leaders, communities, and their allies. Land rights became a central demand within the broader Indigenous rights movement, with a focus on recognizing and restoring Indigenous land ownership, control, and management.

The 1967 referendum, a pivotal moment in Australian history, provided a mandate for change by amending the Constitution to allow the federal government to legislate specifically for Indigenous Australians. This opened the door for subsequent legal and policy reforms aimed at addressing the historical injustices suffered by Indigenous peoples.

One of the significant milestones in the pursuit of land rights was the establishment of the Aboriginal Land Rights (Northern Territory) Act 1976. This landmark legislation recognized the rights of Aboriginal people in the Northern Territory to claim traditional lands based on historical connection and cultural significance. It paved the way for the return of vast tracts of land to Indigenous ownership and provided a framework for negotiation and settlement of land claims.

The Mabo decision in 1992 marked a historic turning point in Indigenous land rights. The High Court of Australia recognized the existence of native title, overturning the concept of terra nullius and affirming the rights of Indigenous peoples to their traditional lands. This decision acknowledged the ongoing connection of Indigenous peoples to their ancestral territories and set a precedent for future land rights claims.

Following the Mabo decision, the Native Title Act 1993 was enacted to provide a legal framework for the recognition and protection of native title rights. This legislation established processes for negotiating native title claims, ensuring consultation with traditional owners, and balancing the rights and interests of Indigenous and non-Indigenous stakeholders.

Despite these significant achievements, challenges persist in the pursuit of Indigenous land rights. The complexity of the legal framework, the burden of proof required in land claims, and the ongoing conflicts between competing land uses present ongoing obstacles. The negotiation and resolution of land rights issues often involve extensive consultations, cultural mapping, and mediation processes.

The recognition and restoration of Indigenous land rights are not solely about legal entitlements. They encompass broader aspirations of self-determination, cultural preservation, and economic empowerment for Indigenous communities. Land rights provide the foundation for economic development, sustainable resource management, and the revitalization of cultural practices tied to the land.

Indigenous land management practices have demonstrated the importance of traditional ecological knowledge in maintaining biodiversity, protecting fragile ecosystems, and mitigating the impacts of climate change. The recognition of Indigenous land rights allows for the revitalization of these practices and the inclusion of Indigenous voices in environmental decision-making processes.

Efforts towards reconciliation and the resolution of land rights issues continue to be pursued through negotiation, mediation, and collaboration. Native title determinations, Indigenous land use agreements, and joint management arrangements have been established in various parts of Australia, facilitating shared responsibility and coexistence between Indigenous and non-Indigenous stakeholders.

The struggle for Indigenous land rights represents a crucial aspect of Australia's ongoing journey towards reconciliation, justice, and self-determination. It calls for ongoing dialogue, empathy, and the recognition of Indigenous rights and knowledge systems. Respecting and honoring the rights of Indigenous peoples to their ancestral lands are fundamental steps towards a more inclusive and equitable society.

The achievements in Indigenous land rights have provided hope and inspiration for Indigenous communities across the country. They have fostered a sense of pride, cultural revitalization, and the empowerment of Indigenous peoples in their pursuit of social, economic, and environmental justice. The ongoing recognition and restoration of Indigenous land rights are vital for healing the wounds of the past, promoting reconciliation, and forging a shared future based on respect and equality.

# The Whitlam Years: Progressive Politics and Social Reform

The Whitlam Years, spanning from 1972 to 1975, marked a transformative period in Australian politics and society. Under the leadership of Prime Minister Gough Whitlam, the Australian Labor Party government implemented a series of progressive policies and social reforms that left a lasting impact on the nation. This chapter explores the key initiatives and the legacy of the Whitlam era.

Gough Whitlam, assuming office as Prime Minister in December 1972, brought with him a vision for change and a commitment to social justice. The Whitlam government prioritized a broad range of policy areas, including education, healthcare, indigenous rights, women's equality, and urban planning.

One of the central pillars of the Whitlam government's agenda was education reform. The introduction of free tertiary education in 1973 through the abolition of university fees revolutionized access to higher education. This policy aimed to ensure that education was based on merit rather than the ability to pay, opening up opportunities for students from diverse backgrounds.

Healthcare was another area of focus during the Whitlam years. The introduction of universal healthcare, known as Medibank, in 1975 aimed to provide affordable and accessible healthcare for all Australians. Medibank laid the foundation for the current Medicare system, which remains a cornerstone of Australia's healthcare system.

The Whitlam government also made significant strides in recognizing and advancing indigenous rights. In 1973, the government implemented the first national policy of self-determination for indigenous Australians. This policy aimed to empower indigenous communities and promote their rights to land, cultural heritage, and self-governance. The establishment of the Aboriginal Land Rights Act 1976 in the Northern Territory was a notable achievement in indigenous land rights during this period.

Women's equality and gender issues were also at the forefront of the Whitlam government's agenda. The establishment of the Women's Electoral Lobby and the introduction of the Supporting Mothers' Benefit aimed to address gender inequality and provide support for single mothers. The Whitlam government also appointed Elizabeth Reid as the first advisor on women's affairs, highlighting its commitment to women's rights and empowerment.

Urban planning and environmental protection were important areas of reform during the Whitlam years. The government established the Department of Urban and Regional Development to address urban sprawl, promote sustainable development, and improve infrastructure planning. Efforts were made to protect the environment through initiatives such as the Great Barrier Reef Marine Park and the establishment of the Australian Heritage Commission.

The Whitlam government's tenure, however, was not without controversy. Economic challenges, including high inflation and rising unemployment, coupled with political disagreements and the dismissal of the government in 1975, brought an end to the progressive reforms of the era.

Despite its relatively short duration, the Whitlam government left a lasting impact on Australian society. The progressive policies and social reforms implemented during this period set the stage for future developments in areas such as education, healthcare, indigenous rights, and gender equality.

The legacy of the Whitlam years continues to shape Australian politics and public discourse. It serves as a reminder of the potential for bold and transformative leadership to bring about positive change. The reforms initiated during this period have influenced subsequent governments, sparking ongoing debates about the role of government in addressing social issues and promoting equality.

The Whitlam era represents a pivotal moment in Australia's political history. It demonstrated the power of progressive politics and the capacity for government to enact meaningful social reform. The legacy of the Whitlam government remains a source of inspiration and serves as a reminder of the importance of pursuing policies that prioritize the well-being and equality of all Australians.

# Bicentenary Celebrations: Reflecting on Two Hundred Years

The bicentenary celebrations of Australia, held in 1988, marked two hundred years since the arrival of the First Fleet in 1788. This chapter explores the significance of the bicentenary, the events and commemorations that took place, and the reflections on Australia's history and identity.

The bicentenary was a significant milestone in Australia's history, providing an opportunity for reflection, celebration, and contemplation of the nation's journey over the previous two centuries. It was a time to acknowledge the achievements, challenges, and complexities that have shaped the Australian story.

The celebrations were wide-ranging and took place throughout the country. Festivals, parades, exhibitions, and cultural events showcased Australia's diverse heritage and highlighted the contributions of various communities to the nation's development. The bicentenary provided a platform to recognize the achievements of Indigenous Australians, migrant communities, and the broader Australian population.

The bicentenary was not without controversy and criticism. Indigenous Australians and some activist groups highlighted the darker aspects of Australia's history, including the dispossession of Indigenous lands and the impact of colonization. These perspectives challenged the notion of a unified and harmonious celebration, urging a deeper reflection on the complexities of Australia's past.

The bicentenary also spurred discussions about Australia's national identity. It prompted debates about what it means to be Australian, the values that define the nation, and the narratives that shape its history. These discussions encompassed issues such as reconciliation, multiculturalism, and the ongoing relationship between Indigenous and non-Indigenous Australians.

The bicentenary celebrations served as an opportunity to examine Australia's history from various perspectives. It encouraged the exploration of diverse voices, narratives, and experiences that contribute to the nation's collective memory. The reflections on the past aimed to foster a greater understanding of Australia's complexities and the ongoing journey towards a more inclusive and reconciled society.

The commemorations also included initiatives to preserve and promote Australia's cultural and natural heritage. Efforts were made to safeguard historically significant sites, artifacts, and documents. Projects were undertaken to record oral histories, digitize archival materials, and engage in historical research to deepen our understanding of Australia's past.

The bicentenary celebrations allowed Australians to reflect on the progress made as a nation and to acknowledge the challenges that lie ahead. It was an occasion to reaffirm commitments to social justice, reconciliation, and environmental sustainability. The celebrations served as a reminder of the responsibility to learn from the past and shape a better future for all Australians.

The legacy of the bicentenary extends beyond the commemorative events themselves. It ignited ongoing discussions about Australia's history, identity, and aspirations as a nation. The reflections prompted by the bicentenary continue to inform public discourse, policies, and initiatives aimed at addressing historical injustices, fostering social inclusion, and strengthening the bonds of the Australian community.

The bicentenary celebrations were an opportunity for Australians to come together, acknowledge the past, and envision the future. They allowed for a nuanced and multifaceted exploration of Australia's history, highlighting the diverse experiences, perspectives, and contributions that have shaped the nation.

As Australia continues its journey, it is essential to reflect on the bicentenary and its lessons. The reflections serve as a reminder of the collective responsibility to build a more inclusive, equitable, and sustainable society. By acknowledging the complexities of Australia's past and embracing diverse voices and narratives, the nation can move forward with a greater understanding of its history and a shared commitment to a brighter future.

# Sydney Opera House: Icon of Modern Australia

The Sydney Opera House stands as an iconic symbol of Australia and a masterpiece of modern architecture. This chapter explores the history, design, cultural significance, and enduring legacy of this world-renowned landmark.

Designed by Danish architect Jørn Utzon, the Sydney Opera House is situated on Bennelong Point in Sydney Harbour. The construction of this architectural marvel began in 1959 and was completed in 1973. Its unique and distinctive design, characterized by its sail-like roofs, has captivated the imagination of people around the world.

The inspiration for the design of the Sydney Opera House came from Utzon's vision of sails billowing in the wind. His innovative and groundbreaking concept was selected from over 200 entries in an international design competition. The design was highly ambitious, combining artistic vision with engineering challenges.

The construction of the Sydney Opera House was a monumental undertaking. The complex design required the development of new construction techniques and technologies to bring Utzon's vision to life. The project faced numerous challenges, including cost overruns, engineering complexities, and delays. Despite these difficulties, the determination and collaboration of architects, engineers, and workers ensured the completion of this architectural masterpiece.

The Sydney Opera House was officially opened by Queen Elizabeth II on October 20, 1973. Since then, it has become an instantly recognizable symbol of Australia and an iconic landmark of Sydney. It has achieved UNESCO World Heritage status, recognizing its outstanding cultural and architectural significance.

The Sydney Opera House is not just a visually stunning structure; it is a thriving center for the performing arts. Its multiple performance venues, including the Concert Hall, Opera Theatre, Drama Theatre, and Utzon Room, host a wide range of artistic and cultural events. The Opera House is renowned for its diverse program, featuring opera, ballet, theater, orchestral performances, contemporary music, and more.

The Sydney Opera House has played host to some of the world's most celebrated artists, musicians, and performers. It has welcomed renowned opera singers, acclaimed theater troupes, international orchestras, and iconic performers from various genres. The venue's acoustics and architectural design contribute to the exceptional experience for both performers and audiences.

Beyond its cultural significance, the Sydney Opera House is an economic driver for the city of Sydney and Australia as a whole. It attracts millions of visitors each year, contributing to tourism and supporting local businesses. The iconic image of the Sydney Opera House has become synonymous with Australia, drawing visitors from around the globe.

The Sydney Opera House has also become a symbol of Australia's cultural diversity and inclusivity. It embraces a wide range of artistic genres, promotes emerging talents, and encourages collaborations across different art forms. It serves as a platform for indigenous performers, multicultural expressions, and thought-provoking artistic endeavors.

The enduring legacy of the Sydney Opera House reaches far beyond its architectural beauty and cultural prominence. It has inspired generations of architects, designers, and artists around the world. Its impact on the field of architecture and its influence on the appreciation of design cannot be overstated.

The Sydney Opera House stands as a testament to the power of human creativity, innovation, and collaboration. It represents the bold aspirations of a nation seeking to establish its cultural identity on the world stage. It is a reminder of the value of investing in arts and culture, as they contribute to the enrichment of societies and the celebration of human expression.

As the Sydney Opera House continues to enchant visitors and inspire artists, it remains an enduring symbol of modern Australia. Its sails continue to grace the Sydney skyline, evoking a sense of awe, admiration, and pride. The Sydney Opera House is a testament to the transformative power of architecture and its capacity to shape the cultural fabric of a nation.

# The Great Barrier Reef: Underwater Wonderland

The Great Barrier Reef is a natural wonder of the world, renowned for its stunning beauty, biodiversity, and ecological significance. This chapter explores the rich marine ecosystem, the challenges it faces, and the importance of preserving this underwater paradise.

Stretching over 2,300 kilometers along the northeastern coast of Australia, the Great Barrier Reef is the largest coral reef system on the planet. It is composed of thousands of individual reefs and islands, collectively forming an intricate and diverse ecosystem.

The Great Barrier Reef is home to an incredible array of marine life, including over 1,500 species of fish, 600 types of coral, and countless other organisms. It supports a complex food web, with various species relying on the reef for survival. The reef's vibrant colors, intricate structures, and abundant marine life make it a haven for divers, snorkelers, and nature enthusiasts from around the world.

The reef's corals are the backbone of this magnificent ecosystem. These colonial organisms, made up of tiny polyps, create calcium carbonate structures that form the basis of the reef's complex formations. Coral reefs are not only beautiful but also provide essential habitat for numerous species, including fish, turtles, sharks, and many others.

The Great Barrier Reef is not only a natural wonder but also an economic and cultural asset for Australia. It generates billions of dollars in tourism revenue each year and supports thousands of jobs in the tourism and hospitality industries. The reef is also of immense cultural significance to Indigenous communities, who have a deep connection to the land and sea.

The reef's fragile ecosystem faces various threats that pose significant challenges to its long-term survival. Climate change is one of the most significant threats, as rising ocean temperatures lead to coral bleaching and the deterioration of coral health. Increased carbon dioxide levels in the atmosphere contribute to ocean acidification, which further impacts coral growth and survival.

Other factors that threaten the Great Barrier Reef include pollution from agricultural runoff, overfishing, coastal development, and crown-of-thorns starfish outbreaks. These combined stressors can degrade the reef's health, disrupt the delicate balance of the ecosystem, and threaten the survival of many species that depend on it.

Efforts to protect and conserve the Great Barrier Reef are crucial for its future. The Australian government, along with scientific organizations, conservation groups, and Indigenous communities, has implemented various measures to mitigate the threats and promote sustainable management practices.

These initiatives include the Great Barrier Reef Marine Park, which was established in 1975 to protect and manage the reef's ecosystem. The marine park implements zoning and regulation to balance human activities with conservation needs. It also incorporates scientific research and monitoring programs to guide management decisions.

International recognition and cooperation are also vital for the conservation of the Great Barrier Reef. The reef has been designated a UNESCO World Heritage site since 1981, highlighting its outstanding universal value. This recognition brings global attention to the reef's importance and fosters collaboration among countries to address the challenges it faces.

Public awareness and education play a crucial role in preserving the Great Barrier Reef. Efforts to raise awareness about the reef's ecological significance, the importance of sustainable practices, and the need for collective action can inspire individuals, businesses, and governments to take responsibility for its protection.

The Great Barrier Reef is a testament to the beauty and complexity of the natural world. Its fragile ecosystem and unique biodiversity deserve our utmost care and attention. By addressing the root causes of its degradation, promoting sustainable practices, and fostering international cooperation, we can strive to ensure that this underwater wonderland continues to inspire and thrive for generations to come.

# Kangaroos, Koalas, and Wombats: Australia's Unique Wildlife

Australia is renowned for its diverse and unique wildlife, with iconic species such as kangaroos, koalas, and wombats capturing the imaginations of people around the world. This chapter explores the fascinating characteristics, ecological roles, and conservation challenges faced by these emblematic Australian animals.

Kangaroos are perhaps one of the most recognizable symbols of Australia. These marsupials belong to the family Macropodidae and are known for their powerful hind legs, long tails, and pouches. Kangaroos have adapted to the country's varied habitats, including grasslands, woodlands, and forests. They are herbivores, primarily feeding on grasses and other vegetation. Kangaroos are capable of hopping at high speeds, enabling them to cover long distances efficiently.

Koalas, often referred to as "koala bears" (though they are not actually bears), are beloved for their cuddly appearance and laid-back lifestyle. These arboreal marsupials are native to Australia and are well-adapted to living in eucalyptus forests. Koalas have a specialized diet consisting almost exclusively of eucalyptus leaves, which are low in nutrients and can be toxic to many other animals. Koalas have a slow metabolic rate and spend most of their time resting or sleeping in trees. They are known for their distinctive vocalizations and adorable, teddy bear-like appearance.

Wombats, with their stocky bodies and powerful digging abilities, are another iconic Australian marsupial. They are part of the family Vombatidae and are known for their burrowing behavior. Wombats have a robust build, strong claws, and a tough, cartilaginous plate on their backsides, which acts as a natural defense against predators. They are herbivorous and primarily feed on grasses, roots, and bark. Wombats are nocturnal creatures and are often spotted at dawn or dusk.

These unique Australian animals play important ecological roles in their respective habitats. Kangaroos, as herbivores, help regulate vegetation growth through grazing and play a role in seed dispersal. They are also a food source for predators such as dingoes and large birds of prey. Koalas are considered "keystone species" in their eucalyptus forest habitats because their selective feeding helps shape the structure and composition of the forests. Wombats contribute to soil aeration and nutrient cycling through their burrowing activities, benefiting other plant and animal species.

Despite their popularity and cultural significance, kangaroos, koalas, and wombats face numerous conservation challenges. Habitat loss and fragmentation, caused by land clearing, urbanization, and agricultural expansion, threaten their populations. Climate change, with its impact on food availability and increased frequency of extreme weather events, further exacerbates these challenges. Human-wildlife conflicts, such as vehicle collisions and dog attacks, pose additional risks.

Conservation efforts aim to mitigate these threats and ensure the long-term survival of these iconic species. The establishment of protected areas, such as national parks and wildlife reserves, helps preserve critical habitats for kangaroos, koalas, wombats, and other wildlife. Scientific research and monitoring provide valuable insights into population dynamics, habitat requirements, and the impact of conservation interventions.

Community engagement and education are vital for raising awareness about the importance of wildlife conservation and promoting responsible human-wildlife interactions. Efforts to minimize habitat disturbance, manage invasive species, and mitigate threats from roads and urban development contribute to the conservation of these unique animals.

Australia's unique wildlife, including kangaroos, koalas, and wombats, serves as a reminder of the country's natural heritage and the need to protect and coexist with the natural world. Their presence enriches ecosystems, captivates visitors, and fosters a sense of pride and stewardship among Australians. By valuing and conserving these iconic species, we contribute to the preservation of Australia's rich biodiversity and ensure a sustainable future for generations to come.

# Aboriginal Art and Culture: Ancient Traditions, Modern Expressions

Aboriginal art is a profound and vibrant expression of Australia's rich indigenous culture, reflecting ancient traditions that have been passed down through generations. This chapter explores the diverse forms of Aboriginal art, its cultural significance, and the ways in which it continues to evolve and thrive in the modern era.

Aboriginal art encompasses a wide range of artistic practices, including rock art, bark painting, dot painting, sculpture, weaving, and contemporary art forms. These artistic expressions hold deep cultural, spiritual, and storytelling significance for Aboriginal communities across the country. They serve as a means of preserving and sharing cultural knowledge, connecting to ancestral lands, and maintaining a strong sense of identity and belonging.

Rock art is one of the earliest forms of Aboriginal art, with some examples dating back thousands of years. These ancient paintings and engravings can be found in caves, rock shelters, and outcrops throughout Australia. They often depict stories, spiritual beliefs, and the relationship between Aboriginal people and the natural world. Rock art serves as a tangible link to the past, providing insights into ancient traditions and the connection between Aboriginal communities and the land.

Bark painting is another traditional form of Aboriginal art, predominantly practiced by communities in the northern regions of Australia. It involves painting on sheets of bark from trees, which serve as canvases. These paintings depict

Dreamtime stories, creation narratives, and daily life experiences. The intricate designs and symbols convey cultural meanings, spiritual beliefs, and the relationship between people, animals, and the environment.

Dot painting is a distinctive and widely recognized form of Aboriginal art that emerged in the 1970s. It originated in the Central and Western desert regions of Australia and has since gained global recognition. Dot painting involves the use of finely applied dots, representing elements of the natural world, ancestral beings, and ceremonial sites. The intricate patterns and vibrant colors create visually striking artworks that convey stories and spiritual connections.

Aboriginal artists also express their creativity through sculpture, weaving, and contemporary art forms. Sculptures often depict ancestral beings, totems, or animals significant to the artist's community. Weaving, using natural fibers such as grasses and pandanus, produces intricate baskets, mats, and other functional items that carry cultural symbolism. In recent years, Aboriginal artists have embraced contemporary art forms, using various mediums to explore personal and political narratives, cultural resilience, and the ongoing dialogue between tradition and modernity.

The cultural significance of Aboriginal art extends beyond its aesthetic appeal. It serves as a vehicle for cultural transmission, enabling the passing on of knowledge, stories, and spiritual beliefs from one generation to another. Aboriginal art reinforces the connection between individuals, their communities, and the ancestral lands they inhabit. It acts as a source of pride, resilience, and cultural revitalization in the face of historical challenges and ongoing efforts for recognition and reconciliation.

Aboriginal art has gained international acclaim and appreciation for its depth, beauty, and cultural value. It has been exhibited in galleries and museums worldwide, showcasing the talent and creativity of Aboriginal artists. The recognition and sale of Aboriginal art provide economic opportunities for artists and their communities, contributing to cultural preservation and sustainable livelihoods. The evolution of Aboriginal art reflects the resilience and adaptability of Aboriginal culture in the modern era. While rooted in ancient traditions, it embraces new techniques, materials, and themes. Contemporary Aboriginal artists are engaging with global art trends, engaging in cross-cultural collaborations, and using their art to engage with social and political issues.

Efforts to protect and promote Aboriginal art and culture involve respecting the intellectual property rights of artists, supporting ethical and fair trade practices, and ensuring that artists receive proper recognition and remuneration for their work. Cultural institutions, government initiatives, and community-led projects play crucial roles in preserving and promoting Aboriginal art, fostering cross-cultural understanding, and supporting the ongoing vitality of Aboriginal cultures.

Aboriginal art and culture represent a profound and enduring legacy, bridging ancient traditions with contemporary expressions. They offer a unique window into the depth, wisdom, and spirituality of Aboriginal cultures, inviting us to appreciate and respect the diverse heritage of Australia's First Nations people. By valuing and embracing Aboriginal art, we honor the resilience and creativity of Aboriginal communities and contribute to the ongoing celebration and preservation of Australia's cultural tapestry.

# Ayers Rock (Uluru): Sacred Heart of Australia

Ayers Rock, also known as Uluru, stands as a majestic and sacred symbol in the heart of Australia's Red Centre. This chapter delves into the geological significance, cultural importance, and enduring allure of this natural wonder.

Uluru is a large sandstone rock formation located in Uluru-Kata Tjuta National Park in the Northern Territory. It is considered one of the world's most recognizable landmarks and has been recognized as a UNESCO World Heritage site since 1987. The rock rises approximately 348 meters above the surrounding plain and extends several kilometers beneath the surface.

Geologically, Uluru has a complex and fascinating history that dates back millions of years. The formation of Uluru began around 550 million years ago when layers of sediment deposited in an inland sea gradually solidified into sandstone. Over time, geological processes, including erosion and uplift, shaped the landscape, exposing the imposing monolith we see today.

Uluru holds profound cultural and spiritual significance for the Anangu people, the traditional custodians of the land. It is a living testament to their rich cultural heritage and spiritual connection to the land. According to Anangu creation stories, Uluru is the result of ancestral beings shaping the landscape during the Dreaming, a period when the world was formed and spiritual beliefs were established.

The Anangu consider Uluru a sacred place, carrying immense cultural and ceremonial significance. It is part of their cultural identity, providing a connection to their ancestors, land, and spiritual beliefs. Uluru is seen as a repository of traditional knowledge, custodianship, and ancestral spirits. It serves as a tangible link to the Dreaming and the ongoing cultural practices of the Anangu people.

Visitors to Uluru are often struck by its breathtaking beauty and the ever-changing colors it exhibits at different times of the day, particularly during sunrise and sunset. The play of light on the rock's surface creates a mesmerizing spectacle, enhancing the spiritual aura that surrounds this sacred site.

Respect for the cultural and spiritual significance of Uluru is paramount. The Anangu people request that visitors refrain from climbing the rock, as it goes against their cultural beliefs and spiritual connection to the land. Instead, they encourage visitors to experience the rock's magnificence through guided walks, storytelling, and cultural activities that foster a deeper understanding and appreciation of the Anangu's connection to Uluru.

The management of Uluru-Kata Tjuta National Park involves collaboration between the Anangu people and Parks Australia. The park is jointly managed with a focus on conservation, cultural preservation, and visitor experiences that respect the significance of the land. Interpretive signage, ranger programs, and cultural centers provide opportunities for visitors to learn about the land's cultural and natural values.

Uluru has become a symbol of Australia, attracting visitors from around the world who seek to experience its unique beauty and cultural significance. It offers an opportunity for reflection, connection, and learning about the profound spiritual beliefs and cultural practices of the Anangu people.

In recent years, there has been a shift towards greater recognition and respect for the traditional custodianship of Uluru. The decision to close the climb in 2019, based on the wishes of the Anangu people, marked an important milestone in acknowledging the importance of cultural heritage and promoting sustainable tourism practices.

Uluru continues to captivate the imagination and inspire awe in those who visit or admire it from afar. Its striking presence, cultural significance, and natural grandeur make it a powerful symbol of Australia's diverse and ancient landscapes. It serves as a reminder of the deep spiritual connection between people and the land, and the importance of honoring and preserving our shared natural and cultural heritage.

# The Outback: Vast Deserts and Remote Landscapes

The Australian Outback, with its vast deserts and remote landscapes, is a region of immense beauty, untamed wilderness, and a unique way of life. This chapter explores the diverse and captivating features of the Outback, its extreme conditions, rich biodiversity, and the resilience of those who call it home.

The Outback covers a substantial portion of Australia's landmass, stretching across the interior regions of the continent. It is characterized by its arid and semi-arid landscapes, where rainfall is limited and the climate is often harsh and unforgiving. The Outback includes expansive deserts such as the Great Victoria Desert, the Gibson Desert, and the Simpson Desert, as well as vast grasslands, rocky ranges, and ancient river systems.

One of the most well-known features of the Outback is its iconic red earth, a result of the iron oxide-rich soils prevalent in the region. The stark contrast of the red earth against the clear blue skies creates a striking and unmistakable visual landscape. The Outback's vastness and solitude evoke a sense of awe and wonder, with seemingly endless horizons and an unspoiled wilderness that stretches as far as the eye can see.

The extreme climatic conditions of the Outback pose unique challenges for both humans and wildlife. Temperature extremes, including scorching heat during the day and freezing cold at night, are common. Rainfall is sporadic and often unpredictable, leading to long periods of drought. Water scarcity is a constant concern, and water sources are crucial for both human settlements and the survival of wildlife.

Despite its harsh environment, the Outback supports a surprising array of biodiversity. Adapted to the arid conditions, a diverse range of plant and animal species call the Outback home. Spinifex grasses, acacia shrubs, and hardy eucalyptus trees are among the resilient plant species that have adapted to the Outback's aridity. In terms of wildlife, kangaroos, emus, wallabies, dingoes, and reptiles such as goannas and snakes are commonly found. The Outback is also home to unique species like the bilby, the thorny devil, and the endangered yellow-footed rock-wallaby.

Indigenous communities have a deep connection to the land and have inhabited the Outback for thousands of years. They possess invaluable knowledge and survival skills honed over generations, allowing them to thrive in this challenging environment. Their profound understanding of the land, water sources, and seasonal patterns enables sustainable practices and a deep sense of custodianship.

The Outback holds an enduring fascination for both Australians and visitors from around the world. It offers a chance to experience a sense of solitude and tranquility, away from the hustle and bustle of urban life. It provides opportunities for adventure, exploration, and reconnecting with nature on an unparalleled scale.

Tourism in the Outback offers diverse experiences, ranging from guided 4WD expeditions to remote cattle station stays, camel treks, and visits to ancient rock art sites. It provides a glimpse into the unique lifestyle of Outback communities, showcasing their resourcefulness, hospitality, and resilience.

However, it is essential to approach the Outback with respect and understanding. Its remote and inhospitable nature demands careful preparation, including adequate supplies, communication devices, and knowledge of safety protocols. Visitors must adhere to leave-no-trace principles, respecting the fragility of the environment and the cultural sensitivities of Indigenous communities.

The Outback holds stories of exploration, pioneering spirit, and the challenges faced by those who have ventured into its vastness. It is a place where legends have been forged, and where tales of resilience and survival continue to be told.

In the face of ongoing environmental changes and the need for sustainable practices, the Outback calls for responsible stewardship. Efforts to protect its unique ecosystems, support Indigenous land management, and promote sustainable tourism contribute to the preservation of this awe-inspiring landscape for future generations.

The Australian Outback is a testament to the power and beauty of nature, a land of contrasts and untamed wilderness. Its deserts and remote landscapes hold a magnetism that has captivated the imagination of people throughout history. Whether exploring its rugged terrain, marveling at its breathtaking sunsets, or simply embracing the sense of vastness and solitude, the Outback offers a glimpse into the raw and untamed heart of Australia.

# The Sydney Harbour Bridge: An Engineering Triumph

The Sydney Harbour Bridge stands as an iconic symbol of Australia's engineering prowess and architectural splendor. This chapter explores the history, design, construction, and enduring legacy of this remarkable feat of engineering.

Construction of the Sydney Harbour Bridge began in 1923 and was completed in 1932, spanning a total length of 1,149 meters (3,770 feet) and connecting the central business district of Sydney with the North Shore. The bridge was designed by British engineer Dr. John Bradfield and constructed by the firm Dorman Long and Co. Ltd., in collaboration with the government agency New South Wales Department of Public Works.

The bridge's design is a testament to both functionality and aesthetics. Its arch design, inspired by the Hell Gate Bridge in New York, was chosen for its strength, efficiency, and visual appeal. The steel arch spans 503 meters (1,650 feet) and rises 134 meters (440 feet) above the water, making it one of the world's largest steel arch bridges.

The construction of the Sydney Harbour Bridge was a monumental undertaking that required the skills and dedication of thousands of workers. It involved innovative engineering techniques, including the use of movable platforms known as "creepers" that allowed workers to construct the bridge from both ends simultaneously. The arches were built using a combination of riveting and steel fabrication, with each component carefully measured and assembled to ensure a precise fit.

The bridge's construction also presented challenges due to the harsh marine environment of Sydney Harbour. Special coatings were applied to protect the steel from corrosion, and ongoing maintenance and painting programs are conducted to preserve the bridge's integrity and appearance.

The completion of the Sydney Harbour Bridge had a significant impact on the city and its residents. It not only provided a vital transportation link but also became an enduring symbol of national pride and unity. The bridge's opening on March 19, 1932, was celebrated with great fanfare, including a procession of around 1,000 vehicles, an air display, and fireworks. Since then, the bridge has become an integral part of Sydney's identity, featuring prominently in cultural events, New Year's Eve celebrations, and as a backdrop for countless photographs.

The Sydney Harbour Bridge is not just a transportation infrastructure but also a popular tourist attraction. Visitors can climb the bridge's arches, offering breathtaking panoramic views of the city and its picturesque harbor. The bridge's pedestrian walkways provide an accessible way to experience its grandeur and appreciate its architectural beauty up close.

Throughout its history, the Sydney Harbour Bridge has undergone several modifications and enhancements to meet the changing needs of a growing city. The addition of extra lanes, the construction of a railway line, and the installation of lighting systems have improved the bridge's functionality and safety.

The Sydney Harbour Bridge represents a triumph of engineering and a testament to human ingenuity. Its construction demanded meticulous planning, innovative techniques, and the perseverance of countless individuals. Today, it remains an enduring symbol of Sydney's skyline, an architectural masterpiece that unites the city and serves as a symbol of connection and progress.

The bridge's iconic status is a testament to its timeless design and the enduring vision of its creators. It stands as a symbol of the strength, resilience, and unity of the Australian people. The Sydney Harbour Bridge is a testament to the power of human achievement and continues to inspire awe and admiration as one of the world's greatest engineering marvels.

# Melbourne: From Gold Rush Town to Cultural Capital

Melbourne, the capital city of Victoria, has a rich history that spans from its humble beginnings as a gold rush town to its current status as a vibrant and culturally diverse metropolis. This chapter explores the transformation of Melbourne, tracing its journey from a frontier settlement to a thriving cultural capital.

Melbourne's story begins in the 1830s when European settlers arrived in the area known as Port Phillip. The discovery of gold in the 1850s fueled a population boom and transformed Melbourne into a bustling gold rush town. People from all over the world flocked to the region in search of fortune, contributing to the city's rapid growth and cultural diversity.

The gold rush era brought immense wealth and prosperity to Melbourne. The newfound wealth fueled the construction of impressive buildings, including grand hotels, banks, and theaters. Melbourne's architecture reflected the wealth and aspirations of its residents, with Victorian-era buildings adorning the streets. Examples of this architectural heritage can still be seen today in the city's laneways, historic arcades, and landmarks such as the Royal Exhibition Building and Parliament House.

The gold rush also had a significant impact on Melbourne's social fabric. The influx of people from different backgrounds and cultures contributed to a vibrant and multicultural society. Immigrants brought their traditions, customs, and cuisines, enriching the city's cultural landscape. This multiculturalism continues to shape Melbourne's identity as a diverse and inclusive city.

As Melbourne grew, it became a center of commerce, education, and industry. The establishment of universities, such as the University of Melbourne in 1853, and cultural institutions, including the National Gallery of Victoria in 1861, contributed to the city's intellectual and artistic development. These institutions fostered a vibrant cultural scene, nurturing the growth of literature, art, music, and theater.

The late 19th century and early 20th century saw Melbourne further expand and modernize. The construction of major infrastructure projects, such as Flinders Street Station and the iconic Melbourne Cricket Ground (MCG), solidified the city's reputation as a hub of activity and entertainment. The MCG, in particular, has become an iconic sporting venue, hosting major events such as the Melbourne Cup horse race and Australian Rules Football matches.

In the latter half of the 20th century, Melbourne underwent urban renewal and revitalization efforts. The city embraced modernist architecture, and notable buildings such as the Royal Exhibition Building and Carlton Gardens were recognized as a UNESCO World Heritage site in 2004. Melbourne's laneways and alleys were transformed into vibrant cultural hubs, featuring street art, trendy cafes, and boutique shops.

Melbourne's commitment to the arts and culture has propelled it to the status of a cultural capital. The city hosts numerous cultural festivals, including the Melbourne International Arts Festival, the Melbourne Comedy

Festival, and the Melbourne International Film Festival. It is also home to world-class museums, galleries, and performing arts venues that showcase both local and international talent.

The city's love for sports is evident in its strong sporting culture. Melbourne is renowned for its passion for Australian Rules Football, cricket, and horse racing. The annual Australian Open tennis tournament, held at Melbourne Park, attracts tennis enthusiasts from around the globe.

Melbourne's thriving culinary scene is also noteworthy. The city is known for its diverse dining options, ranging from multicultural street food to award-winning fine dining establishments. Melbourne's vibrant café culture is celebrated, with locals and visitors enjoying a cup of coffee in its trendy laneways and bustling neighborhoods.

Melbourne's ongoing growth and development are guided by a commitment to sustainability and innovation. The city has implemented various environmental initiatives, including public transportation improvements, bike-sharing programs, and urban greening projects.

Today, Melbourne stands as a cosmopolitan city that embraces its past while embracing the future. Its rich history, diverse cultural fabric, thriving arts scene, and sporting passion make it a city that captivates both residents and visitors alike. From its origins as a gold rush town to its current status as a global cultural capital, Melbourne's journey is a testament to the resilience, creativity, and entrepreneurial spirit of its people.

# The Great Ocean Road: Scenic Beauty on Australia's Coastline

The Great Ocean Road is a world-renowned coastal drive that winds along the breathtaking southern coast of Australia. This chapter explores the history, natural wonders, and iconic landmarks that make the Great Ocean Road an unforgettable journey through some of Australia's most spectacular landscapes.

Construction of the Great Ocean Road began in 1919 as a project to provide employment for returned servicemen from World War I. The road stretches over 240 kilometers (150 miles) from Torquay to Allansford, hugging the rugged coastline of Victoria's south-west region. Its construction was a significant engineering feat, with workers laboring for over a decade to carve a path through cliffs and dense forests, often using only manual tools and sheer determination.

The Great Ocean Road offers breathtaking vistas of the Southern Ocean, with its dramatic cliffs, pristine beaches, and stunning rock formations. One of its most famous landmarks is the Twelve Apostles, a collection of limestone stacks that rise majestically from the ocean. These towering formations, sculpted by wind and waves over millions of years, create a dramatic and awe-inspiring sight.

In addition to the Twelve Apostles, the Great Ocean Road is home to other remarkable rock formations, such as the London Arch (formerly known as the London Bridge) and the Loch Ard Gorge. These natural wonders showcase the power and beauty of nature, with their intricate shapes and the ever-changing colors of the surrounding waters.

The road weaves through lush rainforests, offering opportunities to explore tranquil waterfalls, fern gullies, and abundant wildlife. Koalas can often be spotted lazily dozing in eucalyptus trees along the road, while colorful bird species add vibrant flashes of movement to the verdant landscape. The Great Otway National Park, located along the route, provides a haven for nature lovers, with its diverse flora and fauna, walking trails, and cascading waterfalls.

The Great Ocean Road is not just a scenic drive; it offers a wealth of recreational activities. Surfers flock to the region to ride the renowned breaks at Bells Beach and other popular surf spots. The region is also a paradise for hikers and nature enthusiasts, with numerous walking trails that showcase the area's natural beauty. Visitors can explore the ancient rainforests of the Otway Ranges, take a refreshing dip in secluded beaches, or simply revel in the serenity of the coastal surroundings.

The coastal towns and villages along the Great Ocean Road add to its charm, offering a blend of coastal hospitality and a laid-back atmosphere. Torquay, the starting point of the journey, is known as the surfing capital of Australia and is home to iconic surf brands. Apollo Bay and Lorne offer picturesque seaside escapes with stunning views, while Port Campbell provides a gateway to the Twelve Apostles and the Shipwreck Coast.

The Great Ocean Road is not just a scenic marvel; it also holds historical significance. The Memorial Arch, located near Eastern View, serves as a tribute to the soldiers who built the road and is a reminder of their contributions during and after World War I. The road itself stands as a lasting legacy of their dedication and sacrifice.

Tourism along the Great Ocean Road has flourished over the years, attracting visitors from around the world who seek to experience the unparalleled beauty of Australia's coastline. The road offers a sense of adventure, a chance to connect with nature, and a deep appreciation for the raw power of the ocean.

Preserving the natural beauty and environmental integrity of the Great Ocean Road is of paramount importance. Efforts have been made to protect the region's unique ecosystems, including conservation programs and sustainable tourism practices. Visitors are encouraged to respect the fragile environment, adhere to designated walking trails, and appreciate the area's cultural and natural heritage.

The Great Ocean Road is a testament to the remarkable beauty and diversity of Australia's coastline. Its panoramic views, iconic landmarks, and rich history make it a must-see destination for travelers seeking to explore the country's natural wonders. As visitors traverse this coastal masterpiece, they are reminded of the extraordinary forces that have shaped the land and the enduring allure of the Great Ocean Road.

# The Blue Mountains: Majestic Wilderness Near Sydney

The Blue Mountains, located just a short distance from Sydney, is a region of unparalleled natural beauty and an escape into the majestic wilderness. This chapter delves into the history, geological wonders, diverse flora and fauna, and cultural significance of the Blue Mountains.

Spanning over 11,000 square kilometers (4,200 square miles), the Blue Mountains region is a World Heritage-listed area that encompasses a vast expanse of eucalyptus forests, sandstone cliffs, deep valleys, and cascading waterfalls. Its name derives from the blue haze that often blankets the landscape, a result of light scattering through the fine droplets of eucalyptus oil in the air.

The Aboriginal people, specifically the Darug and Gundungurra, have lived in the Blue Mountains for thousands of years, and their deep cultural connection to the land is still evident today. They hold the mountains and its valleys as sacred, with numerous significant rock art sites and dreamtime stories associated with the area. It is important to respect the cultural heritage of the Aboriginal people and their ongoing connection to the Blue Mountains.

European exploration of the Blue Mountains began in 1813 when Gregory Blaxland, William Lawson, and William Charles Wentworth successfully crossed the rugged terrain, opening up access to the fertile lands beyond. This achievement paved the way for further exploration and eventually led to the establishment of settlements in the region.

The Blue Mountains is renowned for its stunning geological formations, shaped over millions of years. The sandstone cliffs that dominate the landscape exhibit distinctive features such as narrow canyons, towering rock formations, and breathtaking escarpments. One of the most iconic landmarks is the Three Sisters, a trio of sandstone peaks that rise dramatically from the Jamison Valley, offering a breathtaking view of the surrounding landscape.

Waterfalls are another highlight of the Blue Mountains. The region boasts numerous cascades, including Wentworth Falls, Katoomba Falls, and Empress Falls. These waterfalls, fed by the region's abundant rainfall, create a picturesque display of natural beauty and provide a serene and refreshing retreat for visitors.

The Blue Mountains is a haven for nature enthusiasts and offers a myriad of outdoor activities. Hiking is a popular pursuit, with a vast network of walking tracks catering to all levels of fitness and interests. The well-known Six Foot Track, for example, spans 45 kilometers (28 miles) and follows the historic route taken by Blaxland, Lawson, and Wentworth.

Wildlife is abundant in the Blue Mountains, with diverse species inhabiting the region's forests, cliffs, and valleys. The eucalyptus forests are home to iconic Australian animals such as koalas, kangaroos, and wombats. Birdwatchers can delight in spotting native bird species, including colorful parrots, cockatoos, and the elusive lyrebird, known for its mimicry of other sounds in the bush.

The Blue Mountains is not just a wilderness retreat; it also offers a vibrant cultural scene. The town of Katoomba, considered the gateway to the region, is a hub of artistic expression and creativity. It is home to numerous galleries, music venues, and theaters that showcase local talent and host cultural events throughout the year. The Blue Mountains also holds a significant place in Australia's literary and artistic history. The area has inspired many renowned writers and artists, including the iconic Australian poet, Banjo Paterson. The sublime beauty of the landscape and the sense of awe it evokes have found expression in literature, paintings, and music.

Tourism plays a vital role in the Blue Mountains' economy, attracting visitors from around the world. The region offers a range of accommodation options, from cozy guesthouses to luxury resorts, catering to a variety of preferences and budgets. Visitors can indulge in local cuisine, explore charming villages, and immerse themselves in the tranquility of the natural surroundings. Preserving the ecological integrity and cultural heritage of the Blue Mountains is crucial. Efforts are made to manage tourism sustainably, protect native flora and fauna, and raise awareness of the region's environmental significance. Visitors are encouraged to follow designated walking tracks, respect wildlife, and appreciate the fragility of the ecosystem.

The Blue Mountains stands as a testament to the awe-inspiring beauty of nature. Its majestic wilderness, rich cultural heritage, and abundance of natural wonders make it a destination that captivates the senses and nourishes the soul. A visit to the Blue Mountains is a journey into the heart of Australia's natural heritage, a place where one can reconnect with the raw and untamed beauty of the land.

# The Whitsunday Islands: Paradise in the Coral Sea

The Whitsunday Islands, nestled in the Coral Sea off the coast of Queensland, are a tropical paradise renowned for their pristine beaches, crystal-clear waters, and vibrant marine life. This chapter explores the allure, natural wonders, and recreational opportunities that make the Whitsundays a sought-after destination for travelers from around the world.

The Whitsunday Islands are a collection of 74 islands, most of which are uninhabited and protected within the Great Barrier Reef Marine Park. The islands offer a diverse range of landscapes, from untouched rainforests to secluded coves and towering granite outcrops. Their name, given by British explorer Captain James Cook, pays tribute to the day he first sighted them on Whit Sunday, the seventh Sunday after Easter, in 1770.

Whitehaven Beach, located on Whitsunday Island, is one of the region's most iconic attractions. Its pristine silica sand, stretching over seven kilometers (four miles), is among the purest in the world. The beach's breathtaking beauty, with shades of turquoise and azure waters contrasting against the brilliant white sand, captivates visitors and provides a tranquil haven for relaxation and exploration.

The Whitsunday Islands are situated within the Great Barrier Reef, the world's largest coral reef system. This natural wonder teems with an abundance of marine life, including colorful coral formations, tropical fish, turtles, and even the occasional passing manta ray or whale.

Snorkeling and diving opportunities abound, allowing visitors to immerse themselves in the vibrant underwater world and witness the kaleidoscope of colors that the reef offers.

Sailing is a popular activity in the Whitsundays, with the islands providing a picturesque backdrop for exploring the azure waters. Whether navigating independently or joining a guided tour, visitors can set sail on chartered yachts, catamarans, or even traditional tall ships, experiencing the freedom of the open sea and discovering hidden coves and secluded anchorages.

Several islands in the Whitsundays offer hiking trails that lead to stunning viewpoints and provide an opportunity to explore the lush rainforests and diverse flora and fauna of the region. Hikes to Hill Inlet and Whitsunday Peak on Whitsunday Island offer panoramic views of the surrounding islands and reef, rewarding adventurers with breathtaking vistas.

Hamilton Island, the largest inhabited island in the Whitsundays, is a hub for tourism, offering a range of accommodation options, restaurants, and activities. It serves as a gateway to the region, with regular flights connecting it to major cities along the Australian east coast. The island boasts world-class resorts, golf courses, and a variety of water sports, ensuring that visitors have access to modern amenities and recreational opportunities.

Efforts are made to preserve the natural beauty and fragile ecosystems of the Whitsundays. Sustainable tourism practices, such as the provision of designated mooring areas to protect coral reefs and the implementation of strict guidelines for snorkeling and diving, aim to minimize the impact on the delicate marine environment. Visitors are encouraged to practice responsible tourism by following these guidelines and respecting the pristine surroundings.

The Whitsunday Islands provide a gateway to unforgettable experiences and cherished memories. Whether lounging on sun-kissed beaches, exploring vibrant coral gardens, or sailing through tranquil waters, the Whitsundays offer a haven for relaxation and adventure. The natural beauty, combined with the warm hospitality of the locals, creates an environment where visitors can rejuvenate their spirits and connect with the wonders of the Coral Sea.

The Whitsunday Islands stand as a testament to the remarkable beauty and biodiversity of Australia's natural wonders. Their pristine landscapes, vibrant marine life, and idyllic atmosphere make them a destination that captivates the imagination and entices visitors to return time and time again. The allure of the Whitsundays is a true reflection of the splendor of nature and a reminder of the need to preserve and protect these precious habitats for future generations to enjoy.

# Tasmania: Untamed Wilderness and Historic Heritage

Tasmania, an island state located off the southern coast of Australia, is a land of untamed wilderness and rich historic heritage. This chapter explores the captivating beauty, diverse ecosystems, and cultural significance that make Tasmania a unique and alluring destination for travelers seeking both natural and historical experiences.

Tasmania's natural landscapes are nothing short of spectacular. The island is renowned for its pristine wilderness, encompassing rugged mountains, ancient rainforests, deep gorges, and serene lakes. Its untamed beauty has earned it the reputation as the "Natural State" of Australia.

One of Tasmania's most famous landmarks is Cradle Mountain, located within the Cradle Mountain-Lake St Clair National Park. This majestic peak, surrounded by glacial lakes and alpine heathlands, offers breathtaking vistas and unparalleled hiking opportunities. The Overland Track, a renowned multi-day trek, takes adventurous hikers through diverse terrain and showcases the raw and unspoiled wilderness of the island.

Tasmania is also home to unique wildlife, much of which is endemic to the region. The Tasmanian devil, known for its distinctive appearance and fierce temperament, is an iconic marsupial found only in Tasmania. Other endemic species include the Tasmanian pademelon, quolls, and the Tasmanian wedge-tailed eagle. The island's remote and protected habitats provide a sanctuary for these rare and fascinating creatures.

Tasmania's coastline is equally captivating, with rugged cliffs, pristine beaches, and picturesque bays. The Tasman Peninsula, located in the southeast, offers dramatic coastal scenery, including the stunning sea cliffs of Cape Raoul and the natural formation known as the Tessellated Pavement. The Bay of Fires, on the northeastern coast, boasts pristine white sandy beaches, turquoise waters, and distinctive orange-hued granite boulders, creating a captivating contrast against the blue sky.

Historically, Tasmania has a rich and complex heritage. The island was home to Aboriginal people for thousands of years before European settlement. The Palawa people, comprised of several Aboriginal nations, have a deep connection to the land, and their cultural heritage and stories are an integral part of Tasmania's identity.

European settlement began in 1803, when the British established a penal colony at Sullivan's Cove, now known as Hobart, the capital city of Tasmania. The remnants of the penal colony, including the sandstone warehouses of Salamanca Place and the historic buildings of Battery Point, are reminders of Tasmania's early colonial history. The Port Arthur Historic Site, once a notorious convict settlement, offers a glimpse into the harsh realities of convict life and serves as a testament to Tasmania's colonial past.

The influence of the past can also be seen in the architecture and heritage towns scattered throughout the island. Places like Richmond, with its well-preserved Georgian buildings, and Evandale, known for its charming colonial cottages, transport visitors back in time to the early days of settlement. These towns provide a glimpse into Tasmania's colonial history and offer a tranquil atmosphere where visitors can appreciate the timeless beauty of the surroundings.

Tasmania's cultural scene is vibrant and diverse, with a thriving arts and food culture. The Museum of Old and New Art (MONA) in Hobart showcases contemporary and thought-provoking art exhibitions, while the Tasmanian Museum and Art Gallery provides a comprehensive overview of the island's natural and cultural heritage. The state is also known for its high-quality food and wine production, with the fertile soils and cool climate contributing to the creation of award-winning wines, artisanal cheeses, and fresh local produce.

Tasmania's commitment to conservation and sustainability is evident in its protected areas and national parks, which cover approximately 40% of the island. These protected areas, such as the Southwest Wilderness and the Franklin-Gordon Wild Rivers National Park, are recognized as World Heritage sites, emphasizing the global significance of Tasmania's natural and cultural heritage.

Visiting Tasmania offers a unique opportunity to immerse oneself in the unspoiled beauty of nature and delve into the rich tapestry of history. From the rugged mountains to the picturesque coastline, from the convict ruins to the vibrant cultural scene, Tasmania presents a harmonious blend of natural wonders and cultural heritage. It is a destination that encourages exploration, appreciation, and a deep sense of connection to the land and its past.

Tasmania stands as a testament to the delicate balance between preserving its untamed wilderness and celebrating its historical heritage. With its diverse landscapes, unique wildlife, and rich history, the island invites visitors to embark on a journey of discovery, to witness the beauty of the natural world, and to embrace the stories woven into the fabric of its landscapes and communities.

# Australia Today: Challenges, Achievements, and the Road Ahead

Australia, as a nation, has faced numerous challenges and celebrated significant achievements throughout its history. This final chapter takes a look at Australia as it stands today, exploring the current landscape, the pressing issues it confronts, and the opportunities that lie ahead.

Australia is a vast and diverse country, spanning over 7.6 million square kilometers (2.9 million square miles). It is home to a population of over 25 million people, comprising a rich tapestry of cultures, languages, and backgrounds. The nation's multiculturalism is one of its defining characteristics, with a vibrant and inclusive society that embraces diversity.

The Australian economy is robust and diversified, with strengths in sectors such as mining, agriculture, finance, tourism, and education. It has enjoyed a period of sustained economic growth, supported by prudent economic policies, strong institutions, and a highly skilled workforce. Australia is known for its high living standards, quality healthcare system, and accessible education opportunities.

Australia's natural beauty and unique wildlife continue to captivate both residents and visitors. The country is home to some of the world's most iconic landmarks, such as the Great Barrier Reef, Uluru, and the Sydney Opera House. Its diverse landscapes range from the pristine beaches of the coastline to the rugged outback and ancient rainforests, providing a wealth of recreational and tourism opportunities.

However, Australia is not without its challenges. Environmental concerns, such as climate change, water scarcity, and land degradation, present ongoing issues that require careful management and sustainable practices. The preservation of fragile ecosystems, such as the Great Barrier Reef and unique biodiversity hotspots, remains a priority.

Indigenous reconciliation and addressing the historical injustices faced by Aboriginal and Torres Strait Islander peoples are significant ongoing challenges. The country continues to strive towards achieving meaningful reconciliation, recognizing the importance of preserving Indigenous cultures, and addressing socio-economic disparities.

Australia is also grappling with social issues, including affordable housing, healthcare accessibility, and education equity. Ensuring a fair and inclusive society for all Australians, regardless of their background or circumstances, remains a key focus for policy-makers and community leaders.

The country's geopolitical positioning presents both opportunities and challenges. Australia maintains strong diplomatic ties with neighboring countries in the Asia-Pacific region and is a member of influential international organizations. This provides avenues for economic growth, cultural exchange, and collaboration on global issues. However, it also necessitates navigating complex geopolitical dynamics and balancing competing interests.

In recent years, technological advancements and digital transformation have played a significant role in shaping Australia's economy and society. The country has embraced innovation and entrepreneurship, fostering a thriving start-up culture and investing in research and development. This focus on innovation presents opportunities for economic diversification, job creation, and sustainable growth in the digital age.

Australia's political landscape is characterized by a democratic system that encourages public participation, debate, and accountability. Regular elections allow citizens to have their voices heard and participate in shaping the country's future. The democratic process, alongside robust institutions, ensures the smooth functioning of the government and upholds the rule of law.

As Australia looks to the future, it is confronted with the imperative of sustainable development. Balancing economic growth with environmental stewardship, addressing social inequalities, and embracing technological advancements are key considerations. The nation's ability to adapt to a changing world, harness its strengths, and tackle its challenges will determine its trajectory in the years to come.

Australia's story is one of resilience, innovation, and unity. It has overcome challenges, achieved significant milestones, and evolved into a modern and prosperous nation. As it embarks on the road ahead, Australia has the opportunity to build upon its strengths, protect its natural treasures, foster social cohesion, and continue to make a positive impact on the global stage.

# Conclusion

Australia's history is a testament to the remarkable journey of a nation. From ancient times to modern-day, the continent has witnessed the ebb and flow of civilizations, the impact of colonization, and the resilience of its diverse peoples. It is a land of captivating landscapes, unique wildlife, and rich cultural heritage.

Throughout this book, we have explored the multifaceted aspects of Australia's history, from the Indigenous cultures that have flourished for tens of thousands of years to the waves of European exploration and settlement. We have delved into the challenges and achievements that have shaped the nation, from the struggles of early convicts to the fight for Indigenous rights and the pursuit of social equality.

Australia's story is one of complexity and nuance, where different narratives intertwine, and the voices of the past echo into the present. It is a story that reflects the triumphs and tragedies of human endeavor, the ongoing quest for identity and reconciliation, and the resilience of a nation that continually seeks to learn from its past.

As we conclude this book, we are reminded that Australia's journey is far from over. The nation faces new challenges and opportunities, from environmental conservation to social inclusion, from economic growth to technological advancements. The road ahead will require careful navigation and a collective commitment to building a better future.

Australia stands at a crossroads, where the decisions made today will shape the country for generations to come. It is a time for reflection, for open dialogue, and for embracing the principles that underpin a just and equitable society. The diverse voices and perspectives that have been highlighted throughout this book are a reminder that progress is achieved through understanding, empathy, and unity.

As we look to the future, let us recognize the power of knowledge, the importance of preserving our natural and cultural heritage, and the responsibility we bear as custodians of this ancient land. Australia's story is a shared narrative, woven together by the threads of countless individuals and communities. It is in our collective hands to shape the next chapter of this remarkable journey.

May this book serve as a testament to the rich tapestry of Australia's history, an exploration of its diverse landscapes, and an appreciation of the remarkable achievements and ongoing challenges that have shaped the nation. Let us carry the lessons of the past as we navigate the road ahead, with a commitment to inclusivity, sustainability, and the pursuit of a better future for all who call this land home.

The story of Australia is still being written, and it is up to each and every one of us to contribute our part to this ongoing narrative. As we close this book, let us embark on our own journeys of discovery, reflection, and action, and may we find inspiration in the stories, landscapes, and people that make Australia the extraordinary nation it is today.

Thank you for embarking on this journey through the pages of "The History of Australia." We hope that this book has provided you with valuable insights, a deeper understanding of Australia's past, and a renewed appreciation for its diverse heritage.

Your support and engagement as a reader are greatly appreciated, and we would be honored if you could take a moment to share your thoughts by leaving a positive review. Your feedback not only helps us improve as writers but also enables other readers to discover and enjoy this book.

Once again, we extend our heartfelt gratitude for your time, your interest, and your enthusiasm. We hope that "The History of Australia" has left a lasting impression and that its stories will continue to resonate with you long after you have turned the final page.

Printed in Great Britain
by Amazon